IP IN THE
AGE OF AI

IP IN THE AGE OF AI

25 Questions about AI, Copyrights, Trademarks, Patents, and the Future of Human Creativity Answered

JINAN GLASGOW GEORGE
Durham, NC

IP in the Age of AI copyright © 2024 by JiNan Glasgow George

JiNan Glasgow George
P.O. Box 52546
Durham, NC 27717
www.neoipassets.com
Send feedback to jinan@neoipassets.com

Publisher's Cataloging-in-Publication

Names: George, JiNan Glasgow, author.
Title: IP in the age of AI : 25 questions about AI, copyright, trademark, patents, and the future of human creativity ... answered / JiNan Glasgow George.
Description: Durham, NC : JiNan Glasgow George, [2024] | Includes bibliographical references.
Identifiers: ISBN: 979-8-9855625-5-2 (hardcover) | 979-8-9855625-4-5 (softcover) | 979-8-9855625-6-9 (ebook) | 979-8-9855625-7-6 (audiobook)
Subjects: LCSH: Artificial intelligence--Law and legislation. | Artificial intelligence--Economic aspects. | Intellectual property. | Business enterprises--Information technology. | Copyright. | Patents. | Trademarks. | Creative ability.
Classification: LCC: K564.C6 G46 2024 | DDC: 343.0999--dc23

Special discounts for bulk sales are available.
Please contact jinan@neoipassets.com.

Contents

Tell Me What You Think

Let other readers know what you thought of *IP in the Age of AI*. Please write an honest review for this book on your favorite online bookshop.

★ ★ ★ ★ ★

What's Next?

To stay up to date on what *is* changing, you can subscribe to our free email newsletter. You'll get weekly updates, breaking news reports, and industry-insider thought pieces so you always know what is happening and how to take action to preserve and progress your IP rights.

See you at neoipassets.com.

CHAPTER 1

WHEN COMPUTERS HAVE IDEAS

What happens when a computer makes art?

I'm not talking about an artist making a photo collage with Photoshop or drawing something in a digital painting program. And I'm not talking about 3D modeling software either. Those aren't computers *making* art but an artist *using* digital tools to make art.

I'm talking about something quite different.

What happens when a computer generates *its own* art? Or as one famous museum described its latest installation, "What would a machine dream about after seeing the collection of the Museum of Modern Art?"

Unsupervised Artworks

The above question is answered by this image. This picture was taken from an art installation in the Museum of Modern Art (MoMA) by Turkish artist Refik Anadol, entitled *Unsupervised*. It's a global AI data painting that simulates a latent walk among the museum's digitized collection. In MoMA's own words, "As the model 'walks' through its conception of this vast range of works, it reimagines the history of modern art and dreams about what might have been—and what might be to come."[1]

Refik Anadol is not your average artist. He's the forerunner of a new generation of creators who could have emerged only at the dawn of

---

1 - "Refik Anadol: Unsupervised," MoMA, accessed February 16, 2024, https://www.moma.org/calendar/exhibitions/5535.

artificial intelligence. Unlike a typical designer, he uses generative AI to make his artwork. And data is his canvas.

As a pioneer in his field, and the first to use artificial intelligence in a public artwork, Anadol creates at the intersection of humans and machines.[2]

Unsupervised combines Anadol's vision of handling data—within a universe that the program creates for itself—with his approach to data visualization's often neglected opportunity to be a locus for never-ending self-generating contemplation. According to MoMA:

> AI is often used to classify, process, and generate realistic representations of the world. In contrast, Unsupervised is visionary: it explores fantasy, hallucination, and irrationality, creating an alternate understanding of art-making itself. The installation is based on works that are encoded on the blockchain, a distributed digital ledger, which stands as a public record of Anadol's art.[3]

It's extraordinary, a kind of living thing. What he did for *Unsupervised* was input all the works that had ever been displayed at MoMA, then input the sounds from the people who were there, and then input the lighting from the weather outside. Obviously it was more complicated and technical than the way I just described it, but the gist of the effort is that he fed all that data into a generative AI program and then let it make whatever it wanted to make. It's fascinating to watch as it morphs and shifts, forming shapes that are almost recognizable and yet . . . eerie and unlike any art modern or otherwise that we've seen before, at least speaking for myself.

Unsupervised is an example of data in context rendering art. I like to think of it like a digitized M. C. Escher drawing. And as Anadol put it himself, "I view machines as collaborators and push the boundaries of what is possible by utilizing data in a poetic way."[4]

---

2 - Liam McCann, "Refik Anadol: At the Intersection of Art, Science and Technology," Julius Bär, May 15, 2023, accessed February 16, 2024, https://www.juliusbaer.com/en/insights/wealth-insights/our-commitments/refik-anadol-at-the-intersection-of-art-science-and-technology/.

3 - "Refik Anadol: Unsupervised," MoMA.

4 - Liam McCann, "Refik Anadol."

But can *Unsupervised* be considered intellectual property?

Let's start our answer with the source of the question. Anadol himself doesn't really seem to care about copyright or intellectual property. I actually met him in Dubai in March 2023. He was speaking at the Museum of the Future about his work, and I got to record a few little snippets of our one-on-one conversation (with his permission of course), as I was already thinking about what my next book would be after the success of *The IP Miracle*. I found Refik to be warm, approachable, and insightful. So much so that I decided on the spot there in the UAE to open this book with the story of one of his newest creations.

That conversation also compelled me to look deeper into his work. That's when I found out that *everything* he makes these days is AI generated. But especially *Unsupervised*. He didn't train the AI behind that installation or sequence the images it produced or guide or record it. He just fed it the data to train on and let it do its own thing.

He has no copyrights in that work; there's no IP rights in any of it. Anadol's work, and *Unsupervised* directly, may push the boundaries of creativity, but they do not push the boundaries of what intellectual property is.

Then again, who's going to try to replicate it? Well, it's digital, so supposedly someone might be able to copy the file. And Anadol does create NFTs that sell out in less than a minute, which is fascinating. For me, having spent my entire legal career in intellectual property law, it seems counterintuitive. But I like him very much, and he was inspirational to me—going beyond extraordinary—in thinking about our Eclipse IP Futures Conference, and then thinking about this book.

Why *is* he doing this with no IP rights? Having met Refik, I can say from my perspective that he just doesn't seem to care. At all. He's an artist living the life he wants to live, creating the things he loves, and making positive impact globally. He might create NFTs to generate revenue (for income or charity), but he doesn't *have to*. He partnered with Nvidia and Google, and the tech giants appear to act as kind of old-school patrons for him, allowing him to use generative AI without having to consider any typical concerns relating to copyright and IP law.

Refik is an exceptional case because, as we'll see, being reckless with AI and not having concerns for copyright law can have serious consequences.

IP Revoked

Enter Kris Kashtanova.

Kris Kashtanova is a comic book writer and the author of *Zarya of the Dawn*, a short comic about making sense of a postapocalyptic future while accepting one's feelings. Normally, copyright for this kind of thing is fairly straightforward—at the time of a work's creation, the author owns the copyright.

However, Kashtanova used a publicly available generative AI— Midjourney—for the images in the comic. She wrote the script and arranged the panels, but didn't hire an artist. In fact, there was no artist involved at all. Even though she prompted the art program thousands of times to generate the images exactly how she wanted, she didn't actually *make* them.

Kashtanova took these generated images and made a short comic book. And then she submitted it for copyright registration, which she was promptly awarded.

But she failed to disclose that the artwork of her comic was AI generated. You know what happens next, don't you?

Kashtanova went on social media to brag about being the first copyright-registered book with AI art. The United States Copyright Office swiftly came back and revoked her registration, inviting her to comment as to why the AI work *should* be copyrighted. She resubmitted, disclosing how she actually produced the artwork. And she had lawyers argue her case, saying that it took a lot of time and effort for her to prompt the AI, and adjust and tinker with the prompts, and sort through the pieces produced.

The office didn't care—the amount of time spent prompting AI had no impact on rights.

Ultimately, they awarded Ms. Kashtanova partial copyright. According to a letter the US Copyright Office released, "We [the USCO] conclude that Ms. Kashtanova is the author of the Work's text as well as the selection, coordination, and arrangement of the Work's written and visual elements. That authorship is protected by copyright."[5] In other words, the things that Ms. Kashtanova arranged directly—the text on the page, and the actual arrangement of images—were protected by copyright.

Conversely, when it came to the images themselves, the USCO wasn't willing to change their minds or their ruling. "However, as discussed below, the images in the Work that were generated by the Midjourney technology are not the product of human authorship."[6] In the same way you cannot copyright something produced by nature, the USCO has determined you cannot copyright something with only machine and no human authorship. It would be like a sculptor trying to copyright a natural stone arch. While a sculpture he might have carved *would* be subject to copyright protection, a phenomenon "sculpted" by natural erosion wouldn't be entitled to those same protections. And in this case, an image generated by a machine learning program wouldn't be entitled to those protections either.

This legal back-and-forth could have been avoided had Ms. Kashtanova disclosed the content was made using Midjourney. The US Copyright Office had practically said as much in their letter, stating, "Because the current registration for the Work does not disclaim its Midjourney-generated content, we intend to cancel the original certificate issued to Ms. Kashtanova and issue a new one covering only the expressive material that she created."[7]

Kris Kashtanova got her copyright in the end, but that was only after legal headaches fighting the United States Copyright Office. And even that was a consolation prize; she only got *partial* copyright, covering only the aspects of her book that she had direct control over and had directly created, namely the ordering or sequencing of the images and anything she had generated on her own as a human, independent of AI-generated

5 - United States Copyright Office, letter to Van Lindberg, re., Zarya of the Dawn, February 21, 2023, https://www.copyright.gov/docs/zarya-of-the-dawn.pdf.

6 - Ibid.

7 - Ibid.

content. To be clear, even if she had disclosed the AI artwork on her original filing, the partial copyright for her creative works would likely have been granted.

Consolation prizes are not the destiny I want for you.

Why Should You Care?

Maybe you're an artist, picking up this book and wondering how to best protect your art, or how even to implement AI tools yourself. If that's the case, you can clearly see how these stories apply to you.

But my last book was for entrepreneurs, business owners, and innovators. This book is no different. The impact of AI isn't just something artists need to keep in mind. This matters for businesses. If you're an entrepreneur, anyone can use AI-generated content from your website. How could you stop them? How could you protect your content? Even if you register IP rights and it later comes out AI was involved, well then, like in Kris Kashtanova's story, wave bye-bye to those rights, and the protections that come along with them.

So why care about these issues of IP and AI? Because the content on your website, your assets, and more is important. And when it comes to AI and machine learning (ML) technology and IP, some rules are clear, and some are not. And this matters imminently, because IP is important. I wrote a whole book about it.

You *have* to think about IP rights; otherwise anyone can copy you. All your ideas, all the work you put into your business, into developing a new product or process, can just be taken, and someone else can profit off your work. But in this day and age, where you can generate website copy by typing a few prompts into ChatGPT, you have extra precautions to take.

For the outputs you have that are AI generated, you *cannot* register copyrights for them, *and* you have to disclose them to the United States Copyright Office. Kashtanova's mistake was not disclosing that her art was generated by Midjourney, and it's a mistake you don't want to repeat.

When you apply, you have to list the specific elements and everything that was generated by AI, and you have to exempt it from your claim to copyright. But you *can* get copyright on the sequencing of these elements. Remember, Kashtanova was granted partial copyright, not only on what she had written but the *order* in which the individual AI-generated, noncopyrightable images were presented.

This includes content on your website. If you have a website, marketing material, or sales copy generated by ChatGPT, Sudowrite, or some other generative AI tool, you *must* disclose that that content is AI generated. If you want that content subject to copyright protection, however, a human needs to write and edit it. If that's you, wonderful; if it's a contractor, employee, or subcontractor, that's fine as long as they assign you or your business the copyright. Otherwise you don't hold the copyright—they do.

IP laws governing written content also apply to your actual business assets, like products or services you offer. If you used AI to help generate or produce your product, the elements that AI generated are not copyrightable. If you use AI in whatever service you provide, the elements that AI generated are not copyrightable.

So what are the rules? The field of AI itself is still evolving, and so laws around AI are still evolving. We know some of them. We don't know others. But we understand this:

This matters—these rules matter—because IP still matters.

If what I said in my first book—that IP is one of the greatest assets you can acquire for your company—is correct, then AI makes IP rights and following IP rules even more important.

I'm surprised that almost no one with influence in the marketplace has talked about this yet. In fact, I was reading the *Financial Times* on my flight back from Dubai, and that was the first and only time I have seen someone else besides me make this point. Richard Waters, West Coast editor of *FT* based in San Francisco, warned that "the rapid rise of Generative AI threatens to upend the US patent system," noting that "intellectual property laws cannot handle the possibility artificial intelligence could invent things on its own."[8]

---

8 - Richard Waters, "The Rapid Use of Generative AI Threatens to Upend US Patent System," Financial Times, April 26, 2023, https://www.ft.com/content/dc556ab8-9661-4d93-8211-65a44204f358.

What's going on? He went on:

> The US Patent and Trademark Office opened hearings in early May, drawing warnings that AI-fuelled inventions might stretch existing understandings of how the patent system works and lead to a barrage of litigation. The flurry of concern has been prompted by the rapid rise of generative AI. Though known mainly from OpenAI's ChatGPT, the same technology is already being used to design semiconductors and suggest ideas for new molecules that might form the basis of useful drugs.[9]

This goes beyond postmodern art installations at MoMA or comics about self-acceptance. This is impacting *medicine*. This is impacting *computer engineering*. And more.

> For now, such uses of AI do not appear to pose a serious challenge to the patent system **since the technology is being used as a tool to help humans shape ideas rather than operating independently** . . .[10]

Everyone seems to be concerned about job security in the current inflationary, recessionary economic environment, but few seem to care about the IP implications.

You started reading this book because you're one of them.

Who Is IP in the Age of AI For?

This book is for entrepreneurs and innovators in companies who want to leverage generative AI in their work . . . but they have concerns about the uncertainty regarding IP law in this area. It's pretty obvious why—correct answers that you can be *confident* in are hard to find.

So to that end, this book has two uses.

First, you can use this book to find the questions you have and get them answered. Although a lot of IP law surrounding AI is still unclear,

---

9 - Ibid.

10 - Ibid.

there still is settled law that we know. And with my experience as an intellectual property lawyer, I can give you solid knowledge to depend on.

Second, you can come back when you have more questions. That's the thing about IP—if you're using and utilizing it as the powerful asset that it is, then it's never a one-and-done deal. There's always returning to your assets, always reconsidering your position and your IP strategy.

And then, after you've used this book, you can subscribe to the *IP and AI* newsletter at www.Neoipassets.com for the latest updates on what's changing and how that impacts your industry and your very business. At Neo IP, we're on the cutting edge of IP law, keeping track of the effects AI has in this field.

But however you read it, this book will help you understand where we stand now with IP. It will show you how generative AI has challenged this body of law, how it's changing in response, and what the trajectory into the future is. It'll explain what readers do, what to be aware of, and what to avoid when dealing with generative AI.

Let's get started.

CHAPTER 2

WHY IP (STILL) MATTERS

In the age of AI, when you can generate just about anything by typing a sentence to prompt a program, how does that change IP?

That's an important question I will answer in detail over the coming chapters. Right now, a more interesting version of the question is this: In the age of AI, **what does *not* change about IP?**

As this chapter's title claims, IP does still matter, first and foremost. I wouldn't be writing this if it didn't. And I wouldn't have written the previous book either.

Myths, Mistakes, and Miracles Revisited

That first book—*The IP Miracle*—needed to exist because so many entrepreneurs, founders, investors, and owners make uninformed IP decisions that tank their businesses in *days*. Companies hire third-party software developers and don't assign the IP rights to themselves, allowing said software developers to license their "exclusive" product to others.

My book showcased mistakes of both action and inaction. It was about what to do and what *not* to do. It highlighted actionable areas to create multiplier effects and create even greater value than just revenue or customer data alone.

And this was all with intellectual property, with the ideas and knowledge that companies already possessed.

IP is an intangible asset—an idea converted into transferable personal property rights through patents, trademarks, copyrights, service marks, and trade secrets. Intellectual property protection safeguards products and services from imitation, allowing the owner to exclude others from making, using, publishing, selling, and so on; attracts and secures funding from investors; and promotes the overarching commercial success of any enterprise. And yet so few entrepreneurs take full advantage of their one truly unlimited resource—ideas transformed into IP.

So I wrote the book because many entrepreneurs, founders, and investors make fatal IP mistakes that can ruin their competitive advantages, their company's valuation, and the future of the enterprise altogether. *The IP Miracle* ensured that previously uninformed entrepreneurs would finally be able to make IP decisions in an informed way to multiply value and avoid tanking the company.

And that's not an exaggeration. One CEO I saw had destroyed his technology company with a single DIY contract. He planned on licensing out his patents, which itself is not a problem; licensing is a viable way to monetize IP. But instead of contacting an IP lawyer to write a contract that fit his needs, he downloaded a template from the internet and thought he could do it himself.

Normally, patent portfolio licenses grant the licensee a particular patent for a limited field of use. There's language that defines what you can or cannot use the patented technology for and may even specify what markets, geographies, or applications you can use it for.

However, this contract didn't include that, and the CEO didn't add such a list in. What the contract template had instead was a section that said, "You get access to everything *except* what's on this list."

And then he left it *blank*.

One licensee signed the contract and then had access to everything that company did. And, to top it all off, the CEO had then effectively blocked his own company from acting on its own in its already established markets. All so he could get the licensing payments, unintentionally prohibiting his own company from even functioning. He gave his rights away because he had downloaded a contract and thought that he could do it himself.

And the only way out of it would have been to amend the contract. It would have been to get the licensee to agree in writing to change the contract to something more reasonable. The CEO tried to negotiate with that other company, and what did they say? "We don't agree to amend the contract, works just fine for us, we got a great deal out of it!"

It wasn't nice, it wasn't fair, but it was legal. And it could have been entirely avoided had the CEO done his due diligence and not try to handle IP law himself. And it never should have happened! The CEO should have known better; he had multiple law firms that represented the company. He didn't even have them check his DIY contract.

The CEO assumed he could skip the hassle—and the legal fees—and take care of everything himself. But in the end, he had to reach out to the lawyers to try and salvage the disastrous situation he created.

He had investors wanting a meaningful return on the company. He had employees expecting to be able to work and get paid. But the best efforts of his lawyers ended with no results. The worst-case scenario happened. He destroyed his business and gave away all the company's IP assets.

But IP isn't just a risk you have to mitigate, an area of business you need to make sure you get things right on or else you suffer the consequences. My book highlighted actionable areas to create the most valuable assets. IP, when deployed correctly, multiplies your revenue and profits.

What is a patent? What is copyright? What is a trademark? In essence, they're the rights to exclusively use something for a limited time. When a writer copyrights her book, she has an exclusive claim on the text of that book. Nobody else can reproduce it. And she can sell that (or assign it via contract) to a publishing house, giving *them* the exclusive rights in exchange for them giving her royalties.

When a tech entrepreneur develops a new technology and patents it, he has exclusive rights to sell and use that technology. And even if that tech entrepreneur doesn't capitalize on it, even if he doesn't go into business for himself, he can still sell or license out the patent. That's what happened with the 2000–2001 dot-com bust.

Countless companies went belly-up, but their patents didn't expire just because the companies did. So venture funds and companies with security interests in the patent assets sold them. Even after the above company had shuttered, its IP was a surviving tangible asset.

And that's the secret of IP. These assets—copyright, patents, trademarks—are more valuable to acquirers than even to you. And a good IP strategy is about building living assets that make your company more valuable. So you can either enjoy the exclusive rights to the fruit of your labors, or you can sell it off to someone for a hefty sum leveraged in your favor.

My first book goes into that strategizing. Most people don't even realize they *need* an IP strategy, let alone create a faulty IP strategy. They don't realize that *how* you file patents can differ depending on what you want to do with them. Pharmaceutical companies, for example, may not want to fast-track their patents, as the development and commercialization of their IP will take longer, thanks to regulations. Or a company might want to remain in stealth mode and file nonpublication requests when they file . . . but they'd have to know that *when* they file.

And many people don't even realize they can research prior art and identify other patents similar to theirs, which can help aid in getting their patent accepted by making sure the patent is distinct. I once saw a patent on a mask for sleep apnea rejected because it was too close, according to the patent office, to a firefighter's breathing apparatus. Researching prior art would have let us know that fact was something to take into account and something to differentiate from.

In *The IP Miracle*, I describe basic strategy. First, knowing how to use it. Not the product, but the patent itself. You ask yourself the question, "What do I want this patent to do for me?" A patent you intend to utilize for a start-up and a patent you intend to license out are going to function very differently. If someone else can design *around* your patent, why would they bother to pay you to license it from you? If you know you're going to license, you have to design your patent and expand the scope in such a way that it makes it harder to build around without infringing.

Then you have to document it. And document *thoroughly*. You remember when you wrote essays for school, and you got a page count or word length? Patents, or patent templates, have a minimum of a few pages. But that won't cut it. You want to document what the invention is to such an extent that someone should be able to re-create it just by reading your patent application. And not just what it is, but how you got there, and what competitors might do to work around it. And you can't just document from the perspective of the creator; you have to think how someone else might see your creation. A competitor, say, or a user.

Then you have to research existing patents. Examiners usually reject patents on their first time, because you need to prove that what you have is different from other patents already awarded. If your invention has five major elements to it, and the patent examiner can find a patent with two of the five, and another patent with three of the five, then they're ready to reject you for that . . . *unless* you've done your prior research and can differentiate your product from those two prior patents in the application itself. And the only way you can figure that out? Researching prior art.

And then, you need to determine who owns the IP and secure that ownership. If multiple people collaborate on a thing, they all get full ownership. That's not, say, five people, each with a share of 20 percent ownership. It's five people who each own 100 percent of their creations and inventions. If two of those five want to start their own business? They need the other three to sign their ownership over; otherwise the other three can sell it to someone else. Without this step, nobody would fund the company, as the nonsecured ownership would be a gigantic liability.

This also includes employees of the company. I've lost track of the number of times I've seen companies get themselves in hot water because they didn't have nondisclosure agreements or rights assignment with their employees or contractors. One life science company paid a software development group $500,000 for some custom software and made sure to have a confidentiality agreement . . . but neglected assignment of rights. And since software is covered by copyright law, the dev company still held the rights, not the company that hired them. All that business got was a very pricey license to the deliverable.

With patents, there's no second place—miss the date, and it's done. It's a race, with filing and getting accepted as the finish line. You wait too long—you launch, you sell past your grace period (in the US)—then there's no IP for you. No patents. And that's the end result of too many companies.

It's one of those myths I bust in the book, but it makes the most sense. You want to validate your product as early as possible. You get cash on hand, some proof that your product is viable in the market. And maybe you think, like many start-ups do, that you need some inciting incident—like a revenue goal met—before you ought to file. But if you go past that grace period, then you're going to be barred from filing at all!

I discussed how to mitigate this by DIYing some of the patent research and searching in your own market to differentiate your patent claim. It also helps you research your market and de-risk your patent before publishing or sharing publicly (thus starting the countdown to file in the US).

Patents aren't the only area you can go wrong by waiting too long. I've seen too many companies waste money on marketing materials and not making sure to register their branding. Then, when their trademark gets denied, they look at all their promotional materials and realize that it's just wasted money.

But I also discussed how even if you did go to market and didn't file, there's still opportunities. You can change your own work and develop another version, say, based off beta test feedback or planned functions that haven't yet been deployed.

I address other mistakes, other myths about IP, throughout the first half of *The IP Miracle*. Because what not to do matters as much as what to do—and it's a higher priority because it's easier to do than to undo.

I touched on ownership briefly before, but I have a whole chapter devoted to it in my book. The conflict between the life science company and the software company they had hired to develop custom software for them could have been completely avoided had the life science company included an assignment clause in their contract. But they didn't, so we had to maneuver around and use the nondisclosure clause that they *did* include to block the software company from selling the custom product to competitors.

That's one of the four "Nons" I talk about. Nondisclosures prevent others from sharing your IP. Nonuse clauses prevent others from using them. Noncircumvention clauses prevent others from trying to design or work around your IP to file around it. And noncompete clauses prevent third parties, or even your employees, from working in the same area after ceasing to work with you, for a reasonable amount of time.

You need these to protect yourself, because companies are not people. If they can get away with it, they will. Maybe a company is staffed by people with integrity . . . for now. Things change over time, people get hired, fired, promoted, demoted. Profit can get elevated over ethics. I advise using arbitration clauses to avoid these potential conflicts.

I also discuss how to safeguard your patent and to protect your "turf," so to speak. Some companies, the big ones with deep pockets, sue others to monetize their patents. Other companies prefer to use the exclusive rights those patents offer. But I also explain what to do if someone does trespass. I explain what to do with a smaller company compared to a larger company. Sometimes you want a friendly letter. Other times you want to cease and desist.

Most companies don't want to trespass, I found, so starting out aggressive and threatening litigation can hurt you rather than intimidate the other company. In some states, they can even sue *you* for the threat. But some companies—especially bigger tech companies with their infamous "Tech Bro" culture and its disdainful disregard for IP—will infringe. And they happen to be in areas particularly hostile to patent owners.

The IP Miracle discusses the costs of litigation. I discuss litigation funds and how to secure them. But, maybe more importantly, I discuss how to *avoid* litigation. Working *with* someone, or selling or licensing your patent to them, is often less expensive and less time-consuming, as litigation usually drags on for several years. It usually ends in settlement, as everyone just wants to get on with business. And, worst of all, defending a patent is far too much like applying for one; usually by the end of it, the validity of your patent will have been challenged over and over again.

In fact, I even focus on one specific field— software design—and on the fact that much of the culture there seems hostile to patents. Or at best, seems to think they're unnecessary or irrelevant.

Maybe they believe that bigger companies will just steal them. I say that you can always find someone to help enforce high-quality patents—and sometimes that's a competitor of the infringing company, looking to get an edge.

Maybe they believe that patents don't matter anymore and it's all about innovation. I say to look at tech giants; they're the top filers of patents, and if they're spending a ton of money on filing, there's a good reason for it.

Maybe they believe that patent filing distracts from development and innovation. I say that neglecting patents means that you're setting yourself up for disaster down the line. If someone files a patent on what you developed, they can take your idea and legally bar you from using it.

I covered a lot more about IP in my last book, but the main purpose of it was sharing what to do and what not to do in order to best maximize business value via intangibles you might be ignoring. Leveraging copyrights, patents, and trademarks is a part of doing business, even if "Tech Bro" culture wishes it could just ignore it and run roughshod over the whole thing.

But just like I warned people to not ignore IP, don't ignore AI either. It's here to stay. Leverage it as a multiplier for efficiency, idea generation, or predictive analysis. Use it to get ahead . . . but don't use it to replace crucial aspects of your business. You can't afford to DIY it, and you most certainly can't afford to let AI try and DIY it for you.

This book is about both the benefits of AI and the concerns. It's about using AI to multiply your business but also watching out for the unique weaknesses AI brings to the business ecosystem. Both this book and my last book aim to improve valuation for entrepreneurs and ensure that you don't get left behind.

I want to help you move quickly, to know what to do and what not to do. You want to use AI in a way that gives you an edge over your competitors. You don't want an invalid IP, like an AI copyright registration revoked later because it lacked human authorship. You need to be aware of appropriate and inappropriate uses. Because AI magnifies everything, strengths *and* weaknesses. AI, like IP, is a multiplier that exceeds human limitations, but it's still based on human innovation, ideas, and creativity.

Yes, IP Still Matters

Even today, we're still dealing with IP issues. Especially with software. We had a recent client, a venture-backed software company that was designing an app, who was hesitant about patents. It's something we've seen in the tech industry. A lot of developers, especially smaller ones, think that patents are too focused on the past, on preserving what was rather than moving on and innovating.

Normally, VC firms are much more interested in IP protection. After all, why invest in a company whose ideas might get stolen and then blocked by someone who took a design, modified it, and filed a patent first? But in this case, the VC firm itself was not anti-patent, but not pro-patent either. They had the typical software mindset of being first to market.

In the end, we convinced the software company to file a patent. And we were glad we did.

The company planned a big launch on all the app stores. But the week of the launch, they got delisted or blocked. Why? Somehow, the report for the app stores said that their content was identical to existing content, so they couldn't be listed. And just like that, their whole business plan was in jeopardy.

They called us, frantic about fixing this. They'd planned a huge launch and had sunk time, money, and advertising into it. Getting delisted or blocked utterly sidelined them.

Normally, this would be easy for us. We do takedown requests all the time for our clients, using patents, trademarks, and copyrights against infringers. But that's in a court of law. How do you prevent being labeled a copycat and blocked as not being "original" content? How do you prove you're not copying?

Copyright or branding won't help there. Calling your product a different name doesn't matter if the content is the same—the law may see a difference, but the stores don't care. It wasn't a legal infringement we were fighting.

In the end, even just being patent pending provided us the evidence they were not like everyone else.

In this 2023 case, the pending patent application that we filed, that was published, gave the app stores proof of their innovation and uniqueness. This case wasn't about enforcement but about getting into the app stores where potential customers could find them.

Software companies often think that they don't need patents, but almost 60 percent of US patents last year were software related. Big companies like Red Hat and Google see the need to file patents, and file lots of them.

This was our client's hair-on-fire moment that made them realize the value of patents. In this case, it was solid evidence that they weren't copying others and producing a knockoff app. And in this case, we resolved it fast, and they launched successfully.

Branding, customer acquisition, and other excuses *not* to patent don't help in this sort of situation. They're good justifications for not spending money on an IP lawyer, but if you bring up your branding to the app store, they're not going to be swayed.

But even a patent-pending status was enough. It was some evidence of originality that made the stores reconsider their decision and ultimately allowed our client to sell through them. Before, they had claims. With the patent (or even just the application), they were proving their case, and it was resolved in a week.

Often for patents and IP protection, you don't need it until you need it, and when you need it, it's too late.

We have another client whose patent portfolio was valued at over $1 billion by a third party investment bank group. We've worked with the company for over ten years, from start-up to where they are now, with a billion dollars of IP value in a decade via annual investments transforming their technology innovations into exclusive rights via patent applications in a strategic, data-informed process. It's an impressive track record.

Because of our strategic approach, they identified new competitors entering their space as well as large corporations who recently began doubling their investment in patent applications. Using our Patent Forecast software to generate competitive context data, we targeted those competitors, continually blocking new entrants to make our client's IP assets even more valuable. They were the only ones who could operate in their patent-protected space, thanks to how we wrote and designed their patents and other IP.

How did we do it? Well, continually expanding new patent families from early dates let us block rising competition. With our client being the only game in (metaphorical) town, it increased the value of that IP. At this point, they'll likely be acquired within the year due to their IP position—and with their ever-increasing value, they're more of a catch to a larger acquirer.

And the more valuable their IP gets, the bigger they grow. And the bigger they grow, the more consistent their income. And the more vital ongoing IP strategy becomes.

Yes, this takes consistent work. If we weren't consistent, we couldn't have blocked new entrants. This isn't just a file-and-forget process; this is more like marketing. It is *not* a one-off activity. Continuous investment, updating, and aligning with market activity is required. And we do that through predictive analytics.

And there, AI provides our patent analyst teams with valuable foresight.

This strategy stimulates ideas for new assets to file early. These new assets then become other ways of blocking the competition. And with sustained strategic thinking—now enhanced using AI-aided analytics—and focused human innovation, there's the race to file. We're using AI to figure out where the points of entry are, and we direct teams to where they matter the most.

The next major threat is AI on the horizon. Here's your chance to block someone who created something with AI, something that would threaten your market share. Other people will be using AI to try and get an advantage. It is here to stay, and it can be a multiplier like IP . . . but that goes for weaknesses as well as strengths. And IP concerns overlap with AI concerns.

While it is not yet open for AI to take over invention and authorship, that doesn't mean that AI is irrelevant. Like the software company that lost their access to app stores in the story above, this should still be a "hair on fire" moment for you. You need to know your positions and options now.

But there's still a lot that's in flux around AI and IP. That's why I wrote *this* book. To show you what your options are.

And while AI won't replace inventors right now, it does impact IP decisions you will make as you leverage it. Intellectual property includes data assets. This could be the massive amounts of material required to train AIs. And you could even have a proprietary AI that generates data nobody else has. Data itself is an IP asset, and this relationship bridges AI and IP—this is why data still matters, even if we have a ton of it floating around, seemingly ripe for the taking.

Because it's not just quantity. It's not just raw data, but analyzed data integrated with other datasets. It's about identifying which points of data to connect, what patterns to extrapolate, and the insights they reveal that we'd miss, alone, without machine learning. Data considerations in IP are at least as important as patents, trademarks, trade secrets, and copyright.

But remember: AI is only as good as its training data. Big data companies lead in AI simply because they're more massive. They have more data for better training and continuous improvement. It's the same situation with Tesla. The more cars on the road that they have, the more they can provide real-world data to integrate and refine its autopilot and full self-driving systems.

If you can keep others from accessing your datasets, or from using similar ones, you can effectively block out competition from utilizing AI the same way as you do. And software patents are critical in this regard. We've spent this whole chapter showing how IP excludes others from replicating or working around the value you create. With datasets, we can exclude someone using AI to replicate or work around the value you create.

It isn't quite open season for AI to take over invention or authorship. But that may be coming. Get your IP registered while you still can, before potential changes transform the legal landscape. There should be an urgency around capturing IP right now—patents last twenty years from filing.

Now is the time to stake your territory to block AI advances. This should be an incentive to file first, before AI gets a foot in the door. The race to file is more important than ever. Block AI for twenty years if you can. Go for it, humans! And at the same time, use AI right, together with IP, to create multiple revenue and valuation multipliers.

In my last book, *The IP Miracle*, I structured the content as what *not* to do versus what *to* do. Most entrepreneurs approach their IP by doing the wrong things and then not doing the right thing. A lot of this was settled knowledge.

But with AI being so new, most entrepreneurs are approaching AI with uncertainty and trepidation. So this book will be in a Q&A format.

AI and IP can both do what humans cannot. But human ingenuity is their shared foundation.

Let's get to building.

CHAPTER 3

JUST THE FAQS: AI VERSUS COPYRIGHT

E ver heard of GitHub? It's a coding website where programmers can share code and ask for help with programming. Open-source codes are available to use there, and the platform has forums and tutorials and a thriving community of developers.

And, of course, GitHub has automation. Because nowadays, everyone's going, "Oh, let's put a bot on that." So the good people of GitHub decided it would be great if they could train software to write code. There's a lot happening nowadays where you can have a company like OpenAI actually write code, and some of it is actually pretty good. You say what you want the code to do, and the software will write it in the program.

GitHub's version was called Copilot.

If you're a beginner programmer, it's pretty helpful and improves your workflow. But if you're an expert, it can actually take you *longer* if you use Copilot rather than just coding it properly. You spend more time editing the all-right-but-not-good code it produces that you take longer than it would if you had just written it out yourself.

But in order to make Copilot work, GitHub, which has a lot of open-source software on its site, decided that they'd train their AI on everything that was there. Except they didn't exclude—inadvertently or negligently—some of the proprietary code on GitHub that's *not* open source. Without any authorization, they sorta went under the hood and scraped what would otherwise be intellectual property or confidential information, and they used that to train the AI.

What happens is that the AI knows a few new lines of code that are *not* open source, and they start popping up when prompted. So the owners of that proprietary code—anybody affected by what I'm going to call a breach of confidentiality—got involved in a class-action suit. There were so many affected that it *quickly* became a class-action suit.

The argument on the AI side is that they didn't infringe copyright, they just used the proprietary code for training. Problem is, that private code wasn't just used, it was then spat out. The AI was leaking lines of code, and that was how it was discovered. Microsoft and OpenAI are having a similar issue, and mounting a similar defense.

The issues surrounding AI and copyright extend more broadly than just code. Take Getty Images, for example. For those unaware, Getty Images is a large stock photo site. They're in the news right now for taking Stability AI, a software company, to court for scraping (harvesting to train an AI) their over twelve million photo catalog to train its generative AI, Stable Diffusion.

They're also prohibiting AI-generated content from being uploaded to their site. However, they've also demoed their own new generative AI, which they said was not trained on any copyrighted content; in fact, solely on Getty Images' own content.

But the real question underneath this that people haven't answered is about training AI with copyrighted or IP-registered content. Just because it comes from OpenAI or ChatGPT or DALL-E (a text-to-image AI model created by OpenAI) or whatever doesn't mean the end product is okay. Remember Copilot. They got found out because proprietary code started showing up in what the AI was generating.

OpenAI can only give rights to what it has rights to, and if it's using other people's copyrighted material to train and then outputs it? You get a virus that infects everything downstream.

It's not as simple as "no copyright, no problem."

The gist of the answers here is simple. If it's created by AI, it's not a copyrightable creation, whether it's written code, generated text, or images, for the same reason so many other companies, like Getty Images, are working hard to keep their proprietary IP from being part of a training set. AI doesn't create, and to label what AI does as "creating" is a misnomer. It's complexly remixing.

And some of what it may be remixing could be someone else's intellectual property.

Can You Copyright Anything You Create with AI?

No. Only the human-driven sequencing of AI-generated images portion of the work can be possibly considered for copyright registration.

Only humans can generate IP. At least for now, AI cannot invent patentable subject matter, nor can it create anything within the legal definition of "creating." If AI wrote it, artistically rendered it, produced it, or whatever, there's no IP exclusive rights—there's no protection.

Of course, that means that anyone can lift it or copy it for themselves.

Unless you use trademarks (which will be the subject of the next chapter), this content is not copyrightable. Everyone can steal everyone else's "content." The more people that use AI output, the more easily they'll be able to steal from one another content that's commercially viable.

But it's not stealing or unauthorized use if it's free to use—it's in the public domain.

In the end, it still goes back to the race to file, the race to query, the race to deploy. It's the race to market, to have other IP rights around it.

But what does it mean to *create* from an IP law perspective? Machines can't create, only humans can. What does that mean?

When we think about creating, especially in terms of inventions and intellectual property, uniqueness is at the heart of it. *This has never been done before. There's nothing exactly like this.* And, from a patent perspective, *this isn't obvious to others.* To create means that you have put something out there that no one else would have thought of or come up with at the time that you did it.

It's original. It's sort of like God saying, "Let there be light" and the first time the lights came on in the universe. The Big Bang. Well, same idea, maybe a bit less dramatic.

We humans work in a way that's about pattern recognition, sort of like AI's "complex remixing," but we are making contributions for unique thoughts. Think of scientific innovators like Einstein, thinking in a diverging way than anyone else. Making combinations that had never been done.

Even though most inventions are improvements, they still have to be novel, nothing else like it, and they have to be not obvious to someone who's ordinarily skilled. It means you need to think differently, divergently. That's especially true for copyrights. You can't have something that is so similar to someone else's content that it's recognizable as that prior person's work.

Some people might argue and talk about a "collective human consciousness." But it doesn't really manifest like that. Most people aren't plugged into this "collective consciousness," because we're more distracted by everything we're consuming.

Think about someone who watches TV shows all day long. Are they more likely to come up with a unique TV show? No, they're so locked into what everyone's seen, like, for example, the clichéd formula that underlies all sitcoms. To make something original, sure, you need to have seen a certain amount of content, but on the other hand, you need to have some—and this is why I like Refik Anadol's art—*unsupervised* creativity.

Children who grow up with unstructured playtime—running around in the yard, playing in the neighborhood creek—are more likely to make up new games with new rules. But people who are just consuming or are rigidly structured all day long end up lacking the freedom to think in a different way. They lack the flexibility in their minds to go, "This is a square peg. Does it fit in this round hole? How could we make it fit? Does it have to fit?"

They start asking questions that aren't following the rules.

AI itself, to a certain degree just by virtue of being trained on content, is going to be limited by rules. Creativity is knowing (as one of my favorite movies, *The Matrix*, taught me) that some rules are meant to be bent, others broken . . . and sometimes you don't need to make rules.

With AI, the only exception to the rigidity I can think of is Refik Anadol, allegedly. Sure, he started out basically telling the AI, "Do what you want with this data," but it's only beginning to work on being something that we've never seen before. Not because it had ingested the content of everything in MoMA, but because of the continuous new sensor inputs. The noise of the people in the auditorium, the temperature from outside, the level of light from the weather.

We humans get continuous new inputs throughout our day, and then when we sleep, our brains process that and function in a way that's typically not linear. We're making connections, unbound, unrestricted, *unsupervised*. It's why a lot of inventors keep notebooks by their beds.

AI does none of that. It does not create. Thus, anything output by AI has no protection. That means that competitors can lift it.

Can You Copyright Something You Create Yourself but AI Only Helped?

Right now, people don't know how to effectively use generative AI. But that doesn't stop them from trying. Like the example in the first chapter, people have tried and failed to register IP rights for AI-generated content.

Just like "viral" infections can be fatal from "copyleft" clauses (stating that something is free to be modified and distributed as open source, but so must everything derived from it be) in open-source software, AI can prevent you from securing valuable IP rights.

The system of IP rights are rules that our governments create, and then they're rules about how to implement laws. And currently, those rules say you have to disclose what parts were generated by AI. You have to put in what you did and what the AI did. Maybe the inputs are yours and the outputs are AI.

This is kind of what Ms. Kashtanova said. She spent thousands of hours putting in prompts to refine, refine, refine. But she wasn't really creating. She was prompting and sort of molding it all together. If she had shown *her own* painting to the AI and prompted it to iterate off of this, then that painting could be copyright registered, but not the AI generation.

Take a selfie as an example. You take a selfie—that's an artistic creation, one you could copyright register. But if a chimpanzee takes one—not a machine, but a living animal—it's not a person, so no copyright for the chimp. Humans are uniquely capable of creating something that has legal protection.

But what will happen when we have implants? What happens when Neuralink (a company that makes implantable chips for the brain) goes to market and early adopters have access to it and use it for creative purposes? I still think that the human element driving the process will determine what falls under IP law. But that's a conversation that's still unfolding as technology evolves.

Doesn't AI "Create" the Same Way Humans Create?

This is an argument I hear all the time, and we touched on it earlier. If you want to write a science fiction novel, and you read fifty sci-fi novels, then invariably what you've learned from those novels is going to be remixed into your own creation.

Doesn't that mean AI is creating the same way humans create?

There is a sort of consistency there. We recognize patterns, some people more than others, and we make new combinations of known patterns or known components, and that can be inventive.

The difference is that AI has restrictions that we typically don't have. There are patterns of combinations that AI will follow, and follow systematically, that people will not. That may be what makes it more efficient and gives it better computing power.

But we have a flexibility to combine things in a way that isn't systematic or expected. We have divergent thinking. I actually encourage students in my college lectures to use AI to jostle themselves out of a self-inflicted idea rut. It's the same reason why teamwork is interesting—you can get another point of view.

You can have AI give you new thoughts you hadn't considered, and then you can run with it. You can definitely still create in that way. But again, AI may be more efficient, but it's more restricted. You're still taking that idea and adding other parts from your experience, or conversations with other people, dropping this part and welding that part on.

You can tell an AI to come up with a more streamlined design for aircraft, and use biomimicry to do that, say. And the AI will use whatever is in its repository to draw from that. And only what's in its repository. Regardless, none of these ideas can be copyrightable.

And yet the human mind has greater capability than machines do for freethinking. It's like a fractal; the deeper you go, the more complex it gets. The key factor is that it isn't just continuously remixing combinations—our minds are influenced by other sensory inputs.

What Can You Do If Someone Steals Your IP with AI?

Well, with all intellectual property, the good news is that if you participate in the system and register—if you satisfy the requirements and engage with the government to have the exclusive rights to your IP—and you can detect that someone is infringing on those exclusive rights, then you can enforce it in the court system. That's where the property rights and rule of law in the US are advantageous to the extent that we have them. You can either cause the other party to stop infringing through injunctions or have them compensate you for it. If you participate in the system, you have enforcement if you can detect them.

Getty Images is a good example of this, and one I have personal experience with. I hired a third party to do a website for me. It was about flipping the patent system upside down. We had this lovely idea of a mouse and an elephant metaphor throughout the whole site, how IP protects the small guy.

As the team was prepping the site, they found a really gorgeous image of an elephant charging at you. It was from Getty Images. They *meant* to use it as a placeholder and then find a free version or license a cost-effective version, but they forgot to change it out when they published.

Within two days, I got a notification from Getty Images: "You're infringing, take this image down. By the way, you owe us this much money." It wasn't a small sum—close to $10,000.

I was unaware of this, so I called my web design people, who apologized and changed it out, telling me it was meant to be a placeholder. Getty didn't care. They were very aggressive, because that's how they pay the people who make the photography, and they take their cut.

I called Getty; they didn't budge on us owing them money, even when I said there had been no visitors to the site. The fact it had been published had been enough, as they had registered copyrights. I explained I was a small woman-owned business, solo practitioner. I was open to paying a license, and we negotiated a rate for a license.

And then two months later I got another notice from Getty. That's when I found out that the rate I had paid just covered my alleged infringement via the license. I had previously removed the photo from our website in compliance with the license. But it turns out their bots identified a different domain that merely pointed to the old cached version of the website, and there I *did* argue with them, and won on that point. (Pun intended.)

Getty Images isn't the only one who is this aggressive. I have encountered a photographer who watermarks all his work to identify it digitally and is notorious *nationally* for filing lawsuits. In some cases not even sending initial cease-and-desist letters, just directly to suing. Even if you receive one cease-and-desist letter, you may still be sued immediately thereafter. For some lawyers, litigation is just marketing—getting the attention of your prospective customers with a lawsuit (which also creates urgency, since there is a deadline to respond to the suit). Lawyers using this approach won't settle for low rates; you have to pay them more. They have to get a bite of the proverbial apple.

Should Copyright Laws Be Changed Due to AI?

Currently, copyrights last 75 years from the death of the author. And that's if it's an individual. If it's a company, it's 125 years. That includes computer code. It becomes unreasonable. If a programmer writes some code and they pass away, you would have to wait 75 years before being able to use it for anything, including training an AI algorithm. That's ridiculous.

A lot of Silicon Valley and software people have said copyrights should not apply to code because these timelines don't make sense. Forget 75 years; in 7.5 years, that code will be irrelevant. Forget even the old code from early computers in the 1960s and 1970s; you can tell if a website was built in 2010, it looks that outdated.

I personally think that computer code isn't effectively governed by the timelines that IP law established. The original laws said that what you write, what you paint, what you create is what's copyright protectable. Now we have digital works. Is digital art okay, or does that need to be exempt?

The question isn't whether it's created on a computer but rather, is software itself such an unusual thing that transforms so quickly, with different languages that come and go so quickly, that there isn't an effective way to manage IP rights?

But will this be changed?

It takes a lot to change laws in our nation (and other nations). Just looking at the US, I think it could be years before any change to the laws happens. But conversations come up a lot.

If you take away copyright for software code, then blatant copying can happen very quickly. And is that really different from OpenAI generating the code? However, while people like to say that software code moves too quickly, you *can* cover the functionality of code with patents. Though they only last twenty years, which is still kind of long for software, you're not actually locking down the code itself but how it works within a system that has some structure on it, most of the time.

A lot of people say there shouldn't be *any* IP on software, and it should just be a free-for-all. But most people (myself included) don't agree with that. I think limiting copyright time frames on software is an appropriate consideration for Congress to take up and address, because the current time frames end up not being meaningful.

Now, in regards to AI and training, owners can always agree to donate it just like any other IP rights. You can donate these to the public, and you can certainly donate them to AI. So you don't have to wait for Congress.

Developers might say that if you want to use OpenAI or Copilot or something like that, then you have to agree that your code is going to be put back in. Kind of like the open-source contract. In fact, I think this will be dealt with on a contract basis faster than through Congress. And that's perfectly legitimate. You don't have to wait for Congress to change all of IP law, you just have to make it commercially practical that every company that wishes to use the AI software generator has to also contribute back to it, like open source.

That's what I'd propose, at least.

What We Know about AI and Copyright

Anything that AI outputs is not entirely copyright protected even if part of the input was something that you copyrighted and own. Remember the comic in the first chapter. The author only had copyright to the arrangement of the images and the text; the artwork itself was not copyrightable because she hadn't produced it. Only the input you have that appears in the output has copyright protection.

Since AI's output isn't copyright protected, what can you use it for? Things like brainstorming, decision-making and analysis, and problem-solving are still on the table. But you can't do *anything* you plan to publish in public *or* in private (things like trade secrets or contracts, for example). It could also help you *enforce* your IP rights by trawling the internet for any infringement. Getty Images did this; it's how they went after me for a cached copy of a website.

If you want to copyright the output, however, don't use AI—at all. Bottom line.

CHAPTER 4

JUST THE FAQS: AI AND TRADEMARK

The weekend I wrote this chapter, I was at a web meeting hosted by one of my Dubai-based clients.

The entire hour and a half of the meeting was dedicated to leveraging AI in everyday workflow. Whatever everyone's jobs were, how did they leverage AI in carrying them out? We traded stories back and forth, but one stuck out to me.

One of the examples our client gave was coming up with a new logo and how easy it was to use AI to do that. He called on someone in the group and asked, "What's your new product that you're launching that you need a new logo for?"

She gave a couple of details—what the product was, what was happening with it—and voilà, there were four logos. She was using DALL-E, then ChatGPT to transform her comments into technical prompts.

"You are a world-class graphic designer," went the prompt, "and you're specializing in eye-catching logos. I need a new logo for my new project, for educational video content for the facilities management industry. It should be lively, colorful, and dynamic."

That produced two logos that had some common elements but ultimately looked very different. One was a dynamic play button intertwined with a building blueprint, and the next prompt read, "This one's better, but take the text out." Great, done. It took less than five minutes to get the logo done, and she could now apply for a trademark registration for her logo in connection with her services for facilities management education. Really. I am not making this up.

Wait, what?

Wasn't I just saying a chapter ago how you couldn't copyright anything generated by AI? How can you register AI-generated content as a trademark? Why does the creator have to be human for a copyright but not trademarks? Why does the copyright office leap to rescind rights for a comic when they find out that the images are generated by AI, but the trademark office doesn't care how you make your logo?

Copyrights, patents, trademarks . . . one of these things is not like the other. So, what exactly is a trademark? How's it different from copyright?

It can be a confusing point. I recently gave a lecture to a marketing class at a business school in North Carolina. The professor was really confounded by the idea that AI can make trademarks. But it all has to do with the fact that for patents and copyright, the important part is the *content*, while for trademarks, the crucial part is the *activity*.

Copyright is for the content that you've created, and similar to patents, it's for the content that you claim. The idea is that the content is the most relevant part of the exclusive intellectual property rights for patent and copyright.

But for trademarks, it's all about the connection of the symbol to the goods or services in interstate commerce for US marks, not the symbol independently. It's to help consumers identify the source of the goods or services based on the symbol, the logo, or the name that's registered as a trademark. Who cares what it is or if it was AI generated, as long as it's not confusingly similar to anything else in the same goods or services channels of trade.

It doesn't matter how it was generated. Your child could have made it, you could have had work-for-hire people make it. It's not about the trademark itself; it's about what activity is happening and how the symbol, logo, or brand name is connected.

The connection to business and commerce is not something required in patents or copyrights. Trademarks are the only thing that require you to have an activity in order to register. Patents and copyrights you can register in theory; they're just content. You can register and then just sit on them.

In terms of scope and length of time, trademarks can last indefinitely, as long as you continue to make and sell the goods or services. It's the only unlimited exclusive, but you *have* to have commercial activity *and* the use of the mark, whereas with copyrights and patents, you don't have to actually do anything.

Trademarks are different, and maybe even more valuable because, again, if you sell your company, and you have trademarks that are distinctive, and you have products and services that are making money, they're attractive. The larger the company that buys and assumes your footprint, the more valuable those marks will be to their bigger customer base. The larger the company, the larger the scope of the exclusive rights. That's a significant reason that IP assets give a multiplier effect on business value at exit.

Can You Trademark a Logo You Create with AI?

Yes.

We've already established that you *can,* but here's *why* you can . . .

Why are trademarks special protection? What makes them different from copyrights, where AI is a no-go? There's a trade-off. Trademarks demand something else of the applicant that neither copyrights nor patents do. commerce. Trademark registrations require you to explain in detail what the good or service is and how it's being used under the mark. It's why it can't be too close to another trademark and can't be "confusing" to a customer.

Why aren't trademarks affected by AI? Trademark registration doesn't care who created the trademark, they care who *deploys* it, and a human is deploying it. The reason it's not affected by AI is because what's being protected is the good or service being delivered in connection with the mark. The mark doesn't mean anything in isolation. But as soon as you connect it to something in goods or services, then customers recognize the goods and services from your source because of that mark.

So why are trademarks and trade dress (the look and feel of a product that distinguishes it from others) an AI free-for-all zone? Why aren't more companies leveraging AI here?

Trademarks are a domain with potential that isn't being tapped into yet. Maybe some of that is because of the concerns about copyright and AI, but trademarks are a completely different beast. AI could be more effective for trademarks, but it isn't being used that way. So, if it doesn't inhibit registration, why don't more companies use AI to create trademarks?

There may be a couple of reasons, and we'll discuss some of those later, but marketing and branding people should take note. There is an *unlimited* opportunity for AI to shine, if queried properly, and aligned with a company's vision, mission, aesthetics, and all the other intangibles. The trademark domain is still a race to file the best marks, but AI can give you a substantial head start. Or you could be left in the dust as all your competitors innovate and you don't.

AI could generate logos, or even descriptions and more. It's a hot spot not being leveraged because lawyers don't know how to query, say, Midjourney or DALL-E yet to generate usable prompts.

How can companies stimulate the right questions to AI to get outputs they want? I've seen people just throw out things or even get the AI to "role-play" by telling it to pretend it is a graphic designer.

And once you manage to get something generated, how will you know when you have effective marks? Does AI rank options? If it can, can you trust that ranking?

For all the tech and business enthusiasts jumping on the AI bandwagon, I hear almost none of these questions. Trademarks, it seems, are an overlooked space for AI.

Copyrights *can* also apply to trademarks. They do cover artistic works, so they could cover a logo. Slogans and taglines (which we'll cover later) are typically too short. But since some trademarks can be copyrightable, you want to make sure that if you're hiring a person or a company to create one for you, you have the assignment of rights.

If you're using generative AI software, check the terms and conditions, because most of them do change, and they typically say that they do not retain any IP rights. Whatever comes out, there you go. It means that you won't have copyright if AI creates your trademark, but you'll have trademark rights if you use it in connection with your goods or services.

But if you work with a person, it is *essential* that you have that assignment clause. If it's work for hire, they have to agree to assign all rights and interests in the copyrights to you. If you're working with a contractor (and I imagine in the future all contracts with third parties will start requiring this), you are going to want an affirmation or attestation of whether generative AI was used in the process.

What I'm hearing from people who have participated in this in the past are now using generative AI in delivering their work product, and that will affect your ability to register copyrights. You need to have your third parties say whether they used generative AI for logo development. It's kind of an interesting confession. Is the end product worth the same amount?

Maybe the contractor was better at prompting and more creative about engaging with the machine than you are. You're still buying results. But this "confession" is still a question of whether you're paying for human time or not. Or, again, do you have copyrights to register? Trademark and copyright go hand in glove, as sometimes the trademark is used for a slightly different good or service. But for enforcement rights for IP, you would rather not have it be AI generated to ensure you have copyright as well as trademark rights.

To further hammer home how trademarks work . . . On my desk, I have a PEZ dispenser.

On its own, what the heck does PEZ mean? It isn't even a real word! But as soon as you see the goods, you immediately recognize it, the candy with the little dispenser.

What's the trademark? Is it the word? The design of the packaging? There are so many registrations. The word itself, PEZ, in connection with these goods, for one. And you can even see it more clearly on the back of the publishing, the word spelled out with the little candies. That's a mark, a logo. Somebody decided to line up the nasty little sugar tablet–pill things and form the word "PEZ" out of it. That's also registered as a trademark.

But as soon as you even see the plastic dispenser, you know that it's PEZ. It's a nontraditional trademark, just the way it looks. Unique product designs like this could be copyrightable and trademark registrable.

The exact PEZ trademark, as a matter of fact, is for "packaging containers of plastic, namely, cases and boxes for confectionery, and boxes with a dispenser function for confectionery, pastilles and dragees." First use of this was in 1949, and then it was first used *in commerce* in 1953.

The description of the actual trademark itself is "The mark consists of a three-dimensional configuration of candy dispenser being a hollow rectangular box, the word 'PEZ' in a brick design appearing on two sides, ridges appearing on two sides and two oval feet at the bottom." Like I said about patents in my last book, these descriptions need to be exhaustive enough so you know exactly what you're looking at.

But if any of that isn't done by a human being, it doesn't matter. All you have to do is connect it with goods and services in interstate commerce. And then you have it for a long time. PEZ dispensers have been around since 1949. How valuable is that?

But as to who invented the design . . . who cares? It could have been AI (though back then we know it wasn't).

Or take another example, 3M. What does "3M" mean? Nothing, except for what they do and the products they sell. And hypothetically, you cannot duplicate these logos. Another company that wants to sell candy dispensers can't copy and paste the PEZ logo. You can't copy and paste the 3M logo for your own product. Even if they were generated by AI.

Can You Trademark a Tagline, Headline, or Slogan Written by AI?

Yes, you can.

Now, while you might think of trademarks as primarily visual, they are more than just a logo. They can also be a tagline, a headline, a slogan. While copyrights do cover artistic work, taglines typically do not get copyrighted. Trademark-registrable taglines are too short of content for copyright registration, while something like a chapter or text is long enough to be copyrighted.

And you could have ChatGPT create a headline, a tagline, or a slogan that you can trademark. Or even the name of your product or company. A lot of people spend time asking themselves, "What do we call this company? What do we call the product?" You can prompt generative AI to answer these questions for you, telling it that you want something more fanciful or something that combines words from other languages.

You could even come up with domain names, and, assuming nobody's bought it and it's useful, you can go and buy it. It doesn't matter if it's AI generated; it matters if it's acquirable. You can use it as a trademark or even your company name.

Why is this so different from copyright? Why, suddenly, is AI allowed? At the beginning, people get confused because they think all IP is the same. No. Patents and copyrights cover the content that you make. What's the inventive idea you claim? What's the content you've written or visually created? Over here, trademark is about some symbol or mark—whether it's a word or tagline or symbol—in connection with goods or services in commerce by a company. That connection is not required for patents or copyright.

How Can I Use AI to Create Logos, Slogans, and Other Marks for Me to Trademark?

When it comes to trademarks, I like things that are distinctive and memorable and not too generic. So there's a marketing perspective and an intellectual property perspective.

From a marketing standpoint, most people who are experts in that area want to conjure a feeling, a sentiment, a relationship, a faster connection mentally and emotionally with the goods or services. Connection and recognizability are key here.

From the IP side, distinctiveness is better. If it's something you've made up, or something that's fanciful, or something that's even an ordinary word but used distinctively, that works. Think about Apple Computer. The word "Apple" plus anything technical (even support) makes no sense on the surface. What does that even mean? It's completely arbitrary for those goods.

It's the sweet spot, where distinctive and emotional overlap. But generic, which is not good for trademarks, can still work.

We worked with a mark called Vets for Pets. Veterinarians, not veterans. It sounds generic, merely descriptive. It was, but the applicant told me that they liked the name and wanted to keep it, because for years it was plastered on a large billboard off I-95, which funneled a regular stream of new business. However, the trademark office rejected their original claim for being merely descriptive.

After five years, they were able to refile for registration and enforceable exclusive rights (having registered on the supplemental register over the five-year period) and assert to the trademark office that they had developed a secondary meaning, that there were enough customers who recognized the name in connection with these goods and services in interstate commerce that they earned the right to exclude competitors. Ultimately it registered.

Even some generic trademarks can be really strong marks, because they have greater suggestion or descriptiveness to them. And marketing will help reinforce that.

I haven't tried this yet, but maybe try to prompt a generative AI to "pretend you're an intellectual property attorney in the United States of America. Design me a logo that won't be infringing on any other trademarks."

Can AI practice law in this fashion? We already know that AI isn't quite ready for prime time in terms of filing complaints, because it hallucinates and fabricates cases and rules and will cite cases and legal precedent that never happened.[11]

This leads to another issue with AI. Just because AI made it does *not* mean it's free to use. It could be infringing if it's too identical to existing trademarked content. Just because it was created doesn't mean you can register rights. You need clearance.

Why Aren't More Companies Using AI for Trademarks?

A big part of it is that lawyers simply don't know how to use AI. They don't know how to query it. Stories of generative AI citing case law for legal documents from cases that have never existed has definitely scared off a lot of people.

But even if that doesn't scare someone off, how do you even stimulate AI to give you the output you're seeking? How will you know you've nailed it? Well, we just covered some of that.

The other big issue is *clearance*. Too many companies don't think about clearance, but everyone *has* to think about it. Even nonprofits. If AI makes you a mark, you still need to know that you're not infringing before you start using it. Or you might need to ask AI to get you out of a lawsuit.

---

11 - Ella Lee, "Michael Cohen Gave Lawyer Fraudulent Case Citations Generated by AI," The Hill, December 29, 2023, https://thehill.com/regulation/court-battles/4381736-michael-cohen-gave-lawyer-fraudulent-case-citations-generated-by-ai/.

Clearance means your trademark isn't too similar to other trademarks. The USPTO doesn't tell you that you need an attorney to help determine this; you have to pay a lawyer to do it, or you have to go in yourself to ensure that your new mark that AI generated for you is not confusingly similar to anything that's already prefiled or pending or registered.

You have to run research to compare and contrast to what's registered for similar goods and services.

If you're reading this and you work in marketing and you're not scared yet . . . you should be! While attorneys need to clear logos, here is an area where AI can shine, but it's *still* a race to file. And without using generative AI, there's a good chance you're going to be left stalling at the finish line.

So why hasn't this happened yet?

A lot of the ways AI is currently being used right now is superficial. It's for things that either aren't in your ordinary daily activities, or they are the opposite, like note taking or summarization. It's not revolutionary. It's time saving, it's efficiency generating.

Is AI creative? People don't think of it as being creative, and they don't really use it for anything creative. Even someone telling ChatGPT to write them a LinkedIn post . . . Are LinkedIn posts that creative? I'd suggest that most LinkedIn posts are not that inspiring.

But is AI generating a lot of interesting, creative things? Is AI generating podcast content? No, because what does it have to say? It just regurgitates everything that's online and combines it in different ways.

But where do people get stuck? "What's our logo gonna look like? What's our company name? What's our product name?" Why *wouldn't* you try AI?

I personally think that people haven't yet recognized that there *is* some creative leverage to be gained from using generative AI that does not negatively impact IP rights, namely in the trademark sphere.

People don't know how to do it—fine. How do you ask AI to do these things? This prompting to create requires some experimentation. It requires some trial and error, and it requires some experience. I think the ones who spend the most time with it are the most understanding. I think the human imagination can be stimulated by AI, but we need to know how to engage with it. "I want you to think like an expert graphic designer," you might tell the AI.

One area where you can also use AI is in policing for infringement, as with copyrights and photography. You can support your policing efforts with AI and bots just by having them looking for anything that could be confusingly similar in your sector. You can have it watch competitors and provide alerts, but more than that—it could rank threats as low, medium, or high in terms of similarity.

We had a client this past year who found a small competitor who almost lifted all the content from our client's website description and just put a different company name on it.

They were so small, and that's the thing. Sometimes the small ones are under the radar, but in this case it came to our client's attention when there was a big bid or a project that was out, and this tiny company's name came up.

If you have the rights, if your content is copyrightable, and if your trademark is registered, then AI can help enforce it. Have some human elements always, perhaps in the copyright department, so you have something.

What Not to Forget about AI and Trademark

If there's only three things you take away from this chapter, let it be these.

First, trademarks are different from copyright and patents. Copyright and patents do not require activity; you can sit on them without doing anything. Trademarks require that you use them in interstate commerce. On the other hand, copyright and patents require human authorship; trademarks do not. The main concern is activity. So you can definitely use AI to generate trademarks.

Second, just because AI *can* generate a trademark doesn't mean it will get approved. You still need to consider clearance. AI can generate a logo for you, but if it's too confusingly similar to a competitor's mark, it doesn't have *clearance.* This is something everyone, even nonprofits, need to think about, and it's a service a lawyer can provide.

Finally, this should also be a warning. If you're not using AI for trademark strategy and efforts, then you're going to fall behind. You simply don't have enough people and enough time to keep ahead. The business owners who by and large have missed automation are so far missing AI. Their workflow is too reliant on manually and mentally doing things. As time passes, the learning curve gets even steeper and longer.

Now, let's move on to the next type of IP: patents.

CHAPTER 5

JUST THE FAQS: AI AND PATENTS

I 've been ahead of the curve when it comes to AI and patents, thanks to my company's Patent Forecast technology. But how did that start?

Its origin story backs up into *my* origin story in patent law, which goes back to engineering roots. I was a new product research and development engineer for over five years with an industrial company. A lot of the work I was doing there was about the systems and the methods we used. Not just new products, but how we did things systematically and documented them to have standard operating procedures to manufacture, and how to scale them up into production.

In order to transition into patent law, one of the things that I thought about was, "Where is the data I need to inform my advice to clients?" When I launched my practice, and even before when I worked for the patent office, the patent office had all the data. If you wanted data about patents prior to around 1998, you had to physically go to the US Patent and Trademark Office to search on their machines.

They did not launch the free internet access to the patent repositories at USPTO.gov until the late '90s. Until that time, you had to go to the USPTO main library, or you could go to various public libraries—maybe fewer than twelve in number—around the US that were designated repository libraries for the USPTO. And there was one computer at every site to connect you to the data where it was possible to run DOS-like queries to retrieve a list of patent numbers that might match your query.

When they did allow for an automated search from repository libraries, you were using a DOS-like system where you had to enter in some keywords with connected Boolean operators. And then you would just get a list of numbers that matched your query . . . supposedly. And *then* you had to go into the microfilm and microfiche to manually look up every one of those numbers.

I was doing some of that research myself, as I had been an examiner inside the USPTO. At that time, manual research of patent data was required, even though there were digital records or scanned data of the patents that were searchable for USPTO examiners like myself. At that time, you, the researcher, still had to search a physical or printed copy system.

It was only the 1990s, not so long ago, that you were searching through drawers called "shoes" because they were the size and shape of shoeboxes. Even if you made a digital search, you were required to physically go through stacks of printed patent documents in these shoes—for every case. Imagine how often examiners searching the same or similar shoes removed a copy of the patent document for their case, causing other examiners to miss finding it for their own search and examination.

And that was in the mid to late '90s.

Even when they launched USPTO.gov, it wasn't very user-friendly (and some still argue it isn't today), but there was no other place to go to conduct patent research on US-issued patents or published pending patent applications except for another country's patent office.

The reason that all that matters, that all this matters, is that most patents are new combinations of known things. If you know the most similar—the prior—version of a solution to a problem . . . Have you invented something? It's that comparison.

Is it new or novel? Is there anything else like it? Is it differentiated enough to be considered inventive? If so, you apply for a patent. That's what an examiner does—they challenge you. "Do you get a patent? Or do you not get a patent?"

And that prior research, since most patents are new combinations of known components (i.e., improvements), is crucial. That's the point of the patent system.

When I launched my career as a patent attorney in 1999, one of the things I thought was, "I don't want to be running to the repository libraries. Where can I get a better version of this data?" The USPTO wasn't working that well. So I tried all the major data aggregators at the time, such as LexisNexis and Thomson Reuters. They used to charge twenty-five cents per page, or an hourly rate, to have access to their data. And every patent has multiple pages. Data was really valuable, and expensive, if you had that data and could make it available to people who wanted to research it.

And all of a sudden, out came Free Patents Online (FPO) and a few other alternatives. You could run the research for free because the patent office made the data available. Suddenly, the environment changed. Everything was moving toward commodity-free. And remember, those who have more information can better analyze it and combine it in different ways. They were more likely to invent the next patentable invention.

Eventually, even Google launched its own version of free patents online, and now all the data is free. The companies who were charging for data had to start offering a search engine on top of the data to stay ahead of the market evolution. Eventually, most also started offering some form of analytics beyond search results. Some offered visualization of the data as well.

I tried them all, but none worked the way I wanted. I had experience as an examiner and had an idea of the flexibility that I wanted as I began my private practice as a patent attorney.

I decided that we needed to design our own software, and we developed a search engine that was flexible and more effective for every type of query and project. The first generation of our software released under a different company name, Neopatents—deployed cladistics-based algorithms for search, analysis, and visualization applied to patent data. We were creating an evolutionary tree of inventions to find fruitful areas of innovation, to search and explore how technology and science were evolving over time across every industry. We were searching based on the relevancy and the time of evolution in every technological and scientific area, identifying what companies were investing in (since patents can be used as a proxy for research and development) and identifying gaps and opportunities, i.e., what was not yet being done. We were tracking the context around inventions.

Our first generation of patents covered a lot of that, and because patent data is so dense, we got results. But initially, it was just a list of patent numbers, and then you had to manually look at everything.

We needed a way to visualize the search result set, how close they were to each other, and what was different. So we did unrooted tree diagrams, like cladistics, but for patents. It was very useful, because you could see that if you left off one of the components, you had a different dataset and had different companies there compared to including that dataset. It really expedited the analytics as well as the research.

And one of the key factors was how we saw the data, the visualization. This led into the second thing we did, which is why I always call our software "kind of like Google Maps, but for patents." You see, it's important to be able to go from high-level patterns and focus in on more granular patterns, because you get different information at different perspectives depending on where you are in the research and analytics cycle. Patentability questions require one type of research; freedom to operate is another. Same dataset, but different analysis.

When patent data went from being really expensive to a commodity overnight, searching became *the* competitive space. Then it went to needing analytics and has continued to evolve toward predictive analytics. But for us, it was all about visualization.

So Patent Forecast built on that history of Neopatents to understand this idea that things evolve over time. Recency matters, and history matters. And so with Patent Forecast, we have an entirely new form of visualization that's more like radar that moves from the old dates of patents in the center to newer dates of patents toward the perimeter.

That way you can see trends over time, because that's another layer of information you don't see in so-called landscapes, which came after analytics. But even most "analytics" today is what I call patent statistics. How many patents do you have over a given time period? How big is the portfolio? These are so superficial they're almost not helpful. In fact, sometimes they can be deceiving.

That's why we like to think of Patent Forecast software more like the weather. It changes over time. It's not a photo like a landscape, or merely a snapshot in time. We can now see how investment in innovation is changing over time. A lot of companies had even made topographical-style maps based on the number of times a keyword shows up. Who cares? I only care if it shows up once in an independent claim. *That's* important.

Patent Forecast software cuts through that noise. It looks at the evolution of technology over time. In fact, Patent Forecast is the very first visualization software for patents that has a time component that shows not just the number of total patents over time but *granularity* over time. And *then* you can dive into the "street view," to continue the Google Maps analogy. You can look at direct neighbors, see who is inventing what, and read the whole patent.

We also built another workhorse called Patent Matrix software, which was a visualization for claims hierarchical relationship and their content. In the early 2000s, when we invented it, claims research was still being done completely manually inside the patent office. So we continued to evolve with our AI and began to add this ability to have software help us with what used to be all manual searching. We let the data recommend and emerge categories and tell us which things grouped and clustered together, based on all the datasets we had done over such a long time.

This tells you everything about the context. In the drafting and preparation of a high-quality patent, you have to differentiate from prior art. Most patent lawyers, and most companies, don't do this at all. Why?

It's *optional*. There's no requirement to do prior art research. And so most companies and most attorneys don't do it because it would add an extra step and a little bit of cost up front. We always do it because we know the examiner will do it later to our application. We can prepare for it, build in all the arguments and differentiation at the time we draft and file. So that actually saves time and money later and creates a higher-quality asset. It positions you for a greater likelihood of success.

It's not just a race to file the invention, it's a race to file the *highest-quality application* that describes that invention and differentiates it from prior art. So the faster you can search and analyze and understand your differences, the faster you can draft and file.

That data is super useful to everyone from start-up companies to large corporations trying to manage their IP budget and ensure that they're creating quality assets. Companies also need to know what their competition is doing. And so all this data is competitive intelligence. Who has more competitive intelligence? The first to acquire it is usually the winner, because they can act on it first. If you're trying to compete against ten companies and you know what everyone else is doing, or if you know where they have gaps or problems in their portfolio, you can fill them. You win.

There's no second place in patents. You have to file first for the same content. It's a race to file, but there's also a race to get the patent data to understand what competitive and business moves to make. Sometimes, it's not only building your portfolio, it's buying someone else's. So in mergers and acquisition, there's also no second place. Most large corporations grow by acquisition.

You're buying the teams, you're buying their inventions, and you're buying their position in the marketplace. This is why Patent Forecast software and visualization are valuable, why people care about patent data. It's not just companies that are filing but those companies that want a competitive advantage for mergers and acquisitions. And who else cares about it?

Investors.

It turns out that private equity, venture capital funds, and investors also want to find those target M&A companies. They also want competitive intelligence. And even early-stage venture funds want to know if a company is likely to succeed. They can de-risk their investment with this patent data.

You have to file patents before you have public use, which makes patent data a leading indicator. And whoever consumes and analyzes this leading indicator data first wins. There's no second place in getting the patent or buying the other company.

Patent Forecast works for all these stakeholders. Early-stage and growth companies that are innovating and want to know about other patents. Larger corporations that want competitive intelligence and M&A targeting. Investors who want to de-risk their portfolios. That's where we see people getting the most value out of Patent Forecast software.

We offer this as a software as a service (SaaS) because the data changes every week. It's like the weather. I have multiple apps on my smartphone for the weather because I need to look at it in real time. If it's changing, I want to monitor it more closely.

The same goes for Patent Forecast software. You need to know the context, what's around you, and that changes every week. You don't have the time to read or research all of that, but the software will tell you. You can navigate the visual and in just a couple of minutes know what's changed.

Patent rights are the rights to exclude others from commerce, limited monopolies that are granted by the government. And the government gets to decide that conclusion. AI can "invent," as patents are inventive solutions to problems. So AI-generated inventions are still inventive, but as of now, they won't be afforded patent protection in most countries. The one exception so far is South Africa, which just doesn't consider it to be important or weighty enough on their commercial activity for their government to analyze what's patentable or not. They just allow things to be granted patent rights if they follow an administrative process.

AI is best leveraged not in patents themselves but patent research. It's a race to file, and right now, being able to direct your research gives you your best leg up.

Can You Patent an AI-Generated Invention?

No, you can't. You have to be a human. Human beings are uniquely inventors.[12] We generate ideas and transform them into assets. We've covered this.

However, you *can* leverage AI to stimulate your own inventive thinking, which leads us to the next question . . .

How Can You Use AI to Help Draft Patents?

You first have to define "help."

Machines do a lot of things, and machine learning speeds things up. It's computing power, but is it more than that? So far the answer is no, but computing power can be leveraged by humans to invent, so long as there's a human being adding some inventive step to all of it.

Where do we get our ideas from? That's the interesting question to me. Research and analysis, *inspiration* . . . you can automate a lot of that. But if it's in your brain first, it's patentable. You can automate what you want to automate. That's something that inventors should do, because it is still a race to file. Whoever thinks of the new combinations first and files first will win for that content.

We should want to expedite, streamline, and make more efficient some of the research and analytics so we get better at making these new combinations while this is the current state of affairs when AI cannot generate inventions that are patentable.

But that could change. We may be near a tipping point, or on the slippery slope, where AI is granted the rights of a citizen when it comes

---

12 -Davis, Ryan. "USPTO Says AI-Assisted Invention Patents Hinge on Humans." Law360, February 12, 2024. https://www.law360.com/ip/articles/1796756?nl_pk=d9ce393a-4ae1-4645-be4b-877fd1d78066&utm_source=newsletter&utm_medium=email&utm_campaign=ip&utm_content=1796756&read_main=1&nlsidx-=0&nlaidx=0.

to patents. Is it more than computing power right now? No. But this is still an evolving legal landscape.

But besides inventing, can AI help you file patents?

In fact, we worked on something like that. However, it's difficult. Some law companies will make forms you can fill out that then generate legal documents. The problem is, just filling out answers to a question does not create a valuable patent application.

At one time we worked to create a software application we called NeoPPA to draft a provisional patent application by prompting users through the process, with queries that we used for years as patent attorneys. The issue we ran into was that people don't usually respond on their own to queries in a way that's adequate to provide description for patents.

You can use AI to draft that if you have enough content to pull together. If you have the material, AI can help you write it and do transitions and even flag to make sure that every component has a connection and that functionality is described. We always used our Patent Matrix diagrams as a way to outline key components and functions of an invention and then import that automatically into the detailed description section.

That was something we used early on, but what we've found so far—because we know what the requirements of the patent system are, and we have the data on this patentability research to differentiate from prior art—is that most of our writing is an interactive Q&A with the applicant, the inventor. If an AI can ask those questions and the inventor will answer them, then AI can automate the writing of an application.

But there the AI is helping a human by just writing out the human's answers in a workable format. It's like if you have someone who developed a marketing strategy . . . maybe you can get AI to write website code or content, and you pick from it. AI can streamline the documentation of your invention, but the stuff comes from a person. It can prompt you, but you have to answer.

AI can help, and research and documentation can definitely be automated with AI.

Can AI "Invent" Like Humans?

So AI can "invent," but it is more like a hallucination. Randomly generated without purpose. Humans, on the other hand, create in a way completely unlike hallucinations. Invention, in this case, is something that has "never been disclosed" before.

What people do uniquely focuses around the idea of usefulness. It's something I've noticed over twenty-five-plus years. People try to solve problems that matter to *them*, even inside a company. They have been given a problem, or they notice a pain point for themselves. Patents are inventive solutions to problems.

The commercial and practical usefulness of an invention is important to its commercial value. It's not just that you can come up with alternatives for doing something. That just creates a lot of noise in the system, especially when it's a forced consideration of a lot of alternatives. The Chinese Communist Party requires every Chinese national to file in China before any other country. What does that do? It creates a lot of noise in their patent system, because it's not every valuable thing, it's anything you invent that you might want to do something with.

AI can invent, but is the hallucination it invents useful? Is it commercially viable?

The more AI can evolve to answer these questions, great. But right now, people invent things that solve problems for other people. And those are the inventions that are the most valuable. They address real pain points, real problems. And the only way AI could know about these problems is if they are on the web and people complain about them. We can determine when we have a problem ourselves, but AI doesn't have problems.

And legally, only a human can create IP, but as I said before, that may change.

In October 2017, "Sophia," a literal robot, was granted citizenship by Saudi Arabia. Sophia was not only the first robot to receive legal personhood in any country, but she's also en route to becoming the first robotic video-game streamer. Will this become a trend? Will AI be awarded citizenship in other countries?

Whether AI thinks the same way we do, whether it can possess consciousness, is another topic contemplated in recent media. We see that in articles asking whether AI should be given human rights, for example. But even so, AI is at this point not capable of being recognized as an inventor.

We have an AI citizen. If Sophia invented something, could she apply for a patent? If she could, then a lot of IP law would change overnight.

But as of now, in the United States, AI doesn't get awarded patents rights. Some inventors tried to get a patent on behalf of their AI, but it's the human putting the concept in, the human prompting. AI, at this stage, is just a tool. If Sophia's inventors applied for a patent, they could get a patent. But if Sophia applied for a patent, she would be denied.

It's like the chimpanzee who took a selfie—nobody gets any copyright.

Can You Patent AI Software?

Yes, you can, and we have, with Patent Forecast.

I think that one of the highest-growth areas we're seeing right now in patent applications is deploying AI into software across industries. From cybersecurity to medical diagnostics, everything is applying AI to solve problems in every sector. It's typically obvious with software, as that's where AI was born. But remember that in 2022, almost 65 percent of all US patents were software related.

We're seeing it in telemedicine, we're seeing it in cybersecurity, we're seeing it in fintech, we're seeing it in marketing and advertising. Every area that has software. So if that's almost two-thirds of all inventions . . . yeah, AI can help you, and it can be patented as long as it's still novel and not obvious to someone of ordinary skills.

But what does that look like? What does it look like to deploy AI into software? Very often, those software provide analysis over large datasets that allow you to then take action, make a decision, or draw a conclusion from that analysis. With that, you can better understand the landscape, or perhaps even predict things that may occur in the future. And it might even suggest actions to take, to prevent or enhance the likelihood of that happening in the future.

This is a race. It's not just a race to file, it's a race to invent, a race to understand your context. AI is making everything accelerate, and that includes the competition. If you're thinking about it, there's a great chance someone is already acting on it. What steps can you take to take action on your idea?

And as a fair warning, some of the answers in this chapter may change. Keep in touch with us at Patent Forecast (www.patentforecast. com) and NeoIP Assets (www.neoipassets.com), because we monitor this area all the time. We're watching to see how and where things evolve and change. Because once AI can be considered an inventor, that will put a lot of pressure on people to do things more quickly. AI doesn't sleep. You can have it analyze and invent things for you, but you want to make sure that you control the outputs.

And that goes back to the terms and conditions of AI software you use. Do you own the output or not? Even if AI can be considered an inventor, IP rights will still be valuable. It'll just be an arms race in ensuring that you own those rights.

CHAPTER 6

JUST THE FAQS: AI
AND INDUSTRY

W e live in a data economy.
We have sensors to cover everything from autonomous vehicles to smart cities. We have inputs covering more areas of technology and medical diagnostics than ever before. We have self-monitoring wearable sensors that produce a ton of data, and it's more data than anyone could manage with traditional algorithms.

Understanding that we want the *data* to tell us what's happening—instead of us presupposing that some algorithms determine how to analyze that data—is a huge open door for AI into almost every industry. The idea of emergence from data is coming from a unique moment in history.

It isn't just generative AI—large language models like ChatGPT—that can be used in the industry. Models take data from any source, but the larger the data, the better the training, and the better the ability for AI to draw conclusions, see patterns, determine new things, and then give some outputs that are not just insightful but predictive.

And that matters when it's possible to take action or make a change, say, in the settings of a manufacturing environment, or in treatments for a patient, or in management of services within a smart city. In fact, these implementations are beginning to happen but are not yet fully commercialized. It's still very early stage.

The previous chapters in this book have been focused on what AI *can't* do in terms of legally creating intellectual assets that you can protect. But this chapter will be about what AI *can* do. I hinted a few times at some of these possibilities, and I'll discuss them again. But we've focused so much on where it is restricted.

What about where it's unrestricted?

There are a *lot* of impactful areas where AI can amplify and accelerate what we can do today. We've already touched on some of them, like smart cities and manufacturing. Some uses may seem trivial, like sports calls, but others are truly life-changing innovations, like faster and more accurate medical diagnostics through AI-enhanced vision.

Consider wireless telecommunications. Nowadays we just take it for granted. We pick up our phone, we can make a call, and there's plenty of room for us to make a call.

Do you remember the old Verizon commercials? "Can you hear me now?" A lot of that was just about the available bandwidth and who was active in which area. For wireless communications, there's a spectrum that has been allocated—typically in slices—for different companies to provide their services. But now that we have so many wireless things (collectively called the Internet of Things), we've run out of spectrum.

How do you manage that? The only way that you manage it is to analyze all the data in real time to determine what communications are present, who's present, what the purpose of the communication is, and how to prioritize it. Right now, that's given the label of dynamic spectrum sharing. Our government has said that's the only way to manage the wireless communication spectrum going forward.

In order to make all of this work without the congestion and contesting of this wireless space, we *have* to have AI help us. We have to have real-time data that can be analyzed and not just be reactive. If you have low-latency, high-reliability, high-priority communications, like traffic-related messages for autonomous vehicles, you can't wait and then tell the AV to make a change. For medical first responders, you have to know in real time what's happening, what has priority, and how that all fits together.

For us to be able to evolve as a society, not just in the US but globally, we have to be able to manage more and larger datasets in real time and even take predictive actions in a way that's never been done before. It's not possible without AI.

That data is still intellectual property, and the AI action on the data, the analysis of it and the insights and predictive modeling that can ensue, can still be intellectual property as trade secrets. Maybe even patentable subject matter. A lot of the clients I'm working with are deploying AI. There's a huge opportunity, and in each of these situations, it's a very specific high-impact, high-footprint, high-relevance deployment to most businesses.

The ramifications of this are astonishing.

In fact, consider the way I'm telling you this now: in a nonfiction book. What do books do? What jobs do they "do" for readers reading them? One is to demonstrate expertise, to show I know what I'm talking about. Books are also a way to document all your ideas in one place and create a physical representation of your life's work.

You could say a book is a physical capstone for your personal brand and expertise. But apart from that, nonfiction books also convey information. They teach or analyze something.

And AI can generate that much faster. And it can engage with you. If you have a question, rather than taking the time to read to figure out the answer, you can just ask an AI. We've been primed for that. "Google it," or ask Siri.

We're already heading this way, where AI is going to eliminate most nonfiction books because they're just providing information that we have to consume and analyze for ourselves and interpret how it applies to our personal question. And back in my undergraduate student days, to even find a book you had to use a physical card catalog. The level of effort required finding the card for the book, then finding the book itself, and then waiting if there wasn't one of a limited number of copies available.

Remember from the last chapter what happened once patents went online? We didn't have to dig through "shoes" anymore? Nowadays, all we have to do is Google it. Or ask Siri, Alexa, or whatever.

This is already applying to books. Clients of mine are experimenting with ChatGPT and other AI tools, and they'll prompt, "Give me a summary of the top twenty lessons in this book." They don't want to read it; they just want the answer from the book.

What is cut out is the communication side of things. Story. It's what separates good nonfiction books from great ones. Story *needs* to be in them. The sort of book that I believe is defunct is the kind published by most university presses. A typical business-related book might be a collection of mostly well-known stories—ranging from Steve Jobs and Apple to Gutenberg's printing press. These stories are analyzed, with different ideas gleaned from them. And in the entire book, there might be one chapter of actionable advice based on all those stories and their alleged insights.

The entire book should have been published as a short article or white paper, and that would have gotten the entire gist across. AI will probably replace many of the reasons people read nonfiction books because the reasons for writing books already decrease.

And we'll see that pattern repeat itself across industries. Which might lead you to wonder . . .

Will AI Replace Human Workers?

It's the elephant in the room that we have to address—the resistance of people and institutions to adopting AI in their industries. What are the barriers to implementation, and how prevalent are they? They're going to vary across industries, but some are more open to AI implementation than others.

Personally, I think the ship has sailed for banking and finance if there *isn't* AI being deployed for security and cybersecurity. Scanning transactions, patterns of behavior, analytics, fraud detection . . . all of these are areas for easy application. And most of the stakeholders here have an alignment of interest in improving services, in increasing accuracy, and in increasing success.

What about medicine? What AI can do there is see things on imaging where we might not recognize the patterns with our human brains. Not every doctor is good at visual pattern recognition. If you have a radiologist who's supposed to spot breast cancer on a scan but never was a great pattern recognizer, then you're in trouble, even if they did great in medical school. But AI? Here it can do things in minutes or hours that might take months for biotech or genetics graduate students.

The ability to significantly compress analytic times to get actionable conclusions is a huge benefit from AI. Doctors have compressed schedules—how do they even spend enough time listening to the patient, much less going over their whole medical history? If you could input all your medical records and AI could give you time-layered indications of cholesterol increasing or hormonal changes, that's incredibly useful.

It doesn't take jobs from doctors or grad students but rather amplifies computing power to see patterns and anomalies that people cannot necessarily see at all. Or they could see it . . . after months of studying the data that you could have just fed into the AI.

And this could end up detecting things like cancer or genetic malfunctions, aiding in diagnoses that could save lives.

People always talk about automation as machines replacing physical human beings. But a lot of automation in factories has increased safety and let people go on to do other things. AI should enhance safety, improve productivity and efficiency, and deliver higher-quality outputs, whatever the outputs are, whatever the industry.

There are still things that we want to have people do. In the arts and in entertainment, humans cannot be replaced. Some workflow automation, sure. Performing data analysis to improve customer experience, obviously. But *art*?

Can you have AI generate music? Yeah. But is that replacing Taylor Swift? No, because people like her story, and her character, and the fact that she will play in the rain (except in Argentina, when the downpour was too intense). AI hasn't replaced musicians, even though AI can make music.

Taylor Swift is the wealthiest musician among many in her generation, and she's selling the live-in-person thing. Maybe Taylor can cancel her ChatGPT account.

In What Industries Is AI Most Beneficial?

The more data-heavy the industry, the more AI will be beneficial. Not just data streams, but data lakes, or maybe even data tsunamis. Things that are overflowing, overwhelming with data we can't manage.

I think some of these have yet to be deployed. For example, it's unimaginable that our electric power grid will go down in the United States of America in 2024. How does Duke Energy, the largest utility provider in the US, know when my power is out in North Carolina? We call them. It's no smart grid, but the data is overwhelming. It was formerly managed by spreadsheets.

I think any huge data needs AI today. You *need* AI to provide real-time analysis or feedback. As situations and applications require more low-latency and/or high-reliability data, the greater the need for analytics near the source. As technology evolves and Internet of Things (IoT) devices generate more data that requires analysis, integration with other data, and so on, and when you have a high-consequence action, you will have to deploy AI to bring the solutions.

It's not being deployed effectively yet, at least not at scale and not across most industries. Figure out where these data tsunamis are, and seek and deploy AI in your industry, and in your company as well. You can't possibly assess all that data, but AI can, which will give you fast action with competitive advantage. That's the place to have an AI solution for competitive advantage.

Anywhere pattern recognition is crucial is another place AI's machine vision could be used. The analytics machine vision can give you a competitive advantage against others who are still relying on more error-prone and inconsistent human touch. This ranges from sports—think about automated calls on plays, determining if a ball is in or out of bounds—to medical imagery. And while the first example may seem somewhat frivolous, it's the same technology used for medical imaging. AI can discern differences our eyes can't, detecting things instantly that would require extensive human review and diagnostic work otherwise.

But don't just consider things on an industry level; also consider the departments within industries where AI would benefit, and the decisions they are responsible for making. Consulting firms, for example, are at great risk, along with accounting (think about all the DIY tax-return programs out there), even though they may not realize it.

What do consulting firms do now? They throw a bunch of young people on spreadsheets, and *that's* exactly an opportunity to put AI on it and prompt it to figure it out, to ask what the costs are, the major risk issues, and the industry trends.

What Does AI Mean for Patent-Free Zones?

If the most innovative economies have the strictest IP protection, what does that mean for the ability of copyright-free AI inventions to drive prosperity? In other words, Is there any place for AI-generated inventions?

There may be. Consider "patent-free zones" (and for more details, see patentfreezone.com). These are areas, like many countries in the developing world, where patents from other countries (like the US) are not generally filed. In those countries where a patent application is not timely filed in accordance with Patent Cooperation Treaty deadlines, the invention is dedicated to the public—it's free to use in that country or in any country where it wasn't filed. It's an advantage in terms of participation in emerging markets rather than the USA, Western Europe, and elsewhere (think of it like free R&D). These are countries that have less patent protection or participation; with less restrictions, you have more freedom to use existing inventions. You need patent data to unlock this advantage.

In these patent-free zones, AI can make new combinations of new things that you might not have thought of otherwise, in an expedited way. If you can identify a problem to solve, accelerated AI combinatorics is an advantage. It's just a question of implementation. But if you're using AI to innovate and working in a patent-free zone like Ghana or most emerging markets (where you have access to many of the patents filed in the US that are not filed there), you can deploy capital to commercial impact and make sure your technology sells well rather than spending it on R&D. Essentially, it is published research and development—every patent is an inventive solution to a problem. And it is free, as you can use this published work and combine it in new ways, as fast as you can compute it. Essentially, the patents of the developed world provide a how-to manual on a lot of technological and scientific advancement for other countries.

This is more limited in patent-heavy economies, like the US or Western Europe. But for global pre-seed investors like Antler—who are funding thousands of companies—patent-free zones improve returns. How do they review and evaluate so many companies? If they use the same US-centric approach everywhere (like a lot of VC firms tend to do), they miss opportunities.

Different contexts need different strategies to accelerate progress.

This is better than the old "leapfrogging" concepts in business, where developing countries might "skip over" crucial steps in technological development. AI allows emerging economies to rapidly build on others' R&D rather than having to reinvent the wheel themselves. The US body of patents (or any other country's body of patents) becomes a gigantic "how to" manual. Remember, when a patent is improved, it describes exactly how the technology works.

What Won't AI Change in Business?

Relationships, relationships, relationships.

I advise students to just reach out to people on LinkedIn. If the person you want to reach is successful, and you ask in a respectful way, and you're not going to be a time drain to them, they'll answer you. Not everybody, but I find engineers do that a lot.

AI works great for analysis, or even as a personal assistant to manage things. It replaces almost everything *except* relationships. Sure, I've heard and read some things about AI avatars interacting with other avatars to get rid of the uncomfortable cold calling, but it still comes down to people deciding that they're open to meeting new people, or taking new clients or customers.

I do a lot of work with venture capital funds. I invest in them, but I also get a lot of referrals from them. I like that because then they fund companies, they're growing, they're innovative—it's a good fit for us. And we create assets so that if the management team doesn't work out, they can have a soft landing.

But I read an article in the past few weeks about how AI is going to eliminate venture capitalists. It was written by some Silicon Valley guy who's made all his money in venture capital. "It's gone; the door is closed on all you people." There's no more opportunity for new venture funds. Not really? Maybe on data analytics, sure. Maybe on assessing risk, sure.

But on judging people? AI can maybe give some assistance, but at the end of the day, venture capital is about relationships and opening doors for other people to help their company be more successful.

How do you automate relationships? Forget business relationships— what about something like dating apps? I can read your profile and decide if we match, but just because I read your bio, does that mean we're friends? If our bios are great, and we're a perfect fit on paper, but I can't stand talking to you? Or you don't like the sound of my voice? Or I don't like asking questions and hearing what you have to say?

We're not going to have a good relationship—it doesn't matter what the algorithm or AI determines. Nothing changes unless we know each other, and that takes time and interactions. And I don't think you can automate that.

And as more things get automated, the more valuable human engagement will be, and the more time we have to focus on those things that we can uniquely do as humans.

I was listening to something on Instagram from a professor, and he opened with a message for salespeople. Nobody is interested in your product; they're interested in *the product of your product.*

You're not buying an AI bot to buy an AI bot; you're buying it because you want to deliver more in your role in whatever company.

You're buying it so you can be more accurate and get promoted. You're buying it to be more successful in your job and know things ahead of the competition.

We know AI is a product, but what are we really buying? Because we really don't care about AI, we care about what AI gives us. Time is the most important thing. Or insights, or information that we could never get on our own in real time. Or increased impact.

And it lets us spend all the more time on relationship building instead of administrative work.

If you don't think about this, about what product you really want from AI, then you're going to have a harder time implementing and deploying it, because you don't know *why* you got AI. "We're buying AI this year." Okay, what does that mean? What do you get in the industry?

You're buying improved diagnostics to save lives. You're buying customized education to better make the impact you want faster. You're buying reduced time on administrative jobs.

With AI, what else are you buying that you don't have?

CHAPTER 7

JUST THE FAQS: AI AND EVERYTHING ELSE

Between this book so far and its predecessor *The IP Miracle*, you now know the essentials about IP and AI. That said, the field is still evolving. It's slow, as all things are that are directly affected by government regulation. But it's evolving nonetheless. And while we've covered a lot of ground here, there may still be a few questions that may have come up in the past few chapters, prompted by answers to *other* questions.

That's what this chapter is for, to cover the uncovered that hasn't quite fit anywhere else.

What If I Use AI and Just . . . Lie about It?

My husband Francis and I had a conversation about this a couple of weeks ago. He's a musician and has written his own songs, both the scores and the lyrics. He likes some particular types of music—we both grew up in the '80s, so we're fans of that era, though he went through a phase of liking more contemporary music like shoegaze. And one day, he found a new prompt engine, like a MusicGPT.

All he did was prompt a genre and give a few words for the AI to "think" about, and within a minute or two there was music—lyrics generated and several instruments. It gave two or three versions of the lyrics, with different scores in the background, so each version had a different vibe. He could have refined it sooner.

"Doesn't it sound great?" he asked me. "I could just do a lot of music like this and release it as an album."

But then anybody could use it for anything. No copyright on the song. Anybody, I told him, could take it and use it for background in a movie or a video game or even just put the songs on their own albums. And, in fact, he had been critiquing music where people just put new beats or added a new instrumental on the back of someone else's music. "How unimaginative," he would say.

But while he was impressed at first with the AI-generated content, once he realized that that was what it was . . . he came to the same conclusion. It wasn't right. It wasn't . . . *human*. "Read the lyrics," I told him. "They're horrible." Some of them even included the genre name in the refrain.

It was worth nothing.

If you lie about AI-generated content, you can have it revoked, like what happened to Kris Kashtanova. Those rights will be taken away from you, and you won't be able to enforce them.

The whole point of copyright—of having exclusive rights—is to actually be able to keep people out. Or that someone else—a larger company acquiring a smaller company—will value that *they* can keep people out. If there's no fence there, if you can't actually keep people from infringing on your intellectual property, then there's no value there.

And the other thing that can happen if you lie and are caught lying is that you could be precluded from filing any other inventions. They can bar you from using the system if you defraud it.

Even if the output is not subpar and you assign copyright to something (say, some written copy or programming code) and you don't get caught. What happens next?

Well, if it goes to enforcement, then you're screwed. And the whole point of IP law is so you *can* enforce it. If other people step on your content, then why bother with IP? If the graphic novel artist hadn't bragged about using AI to generate her comic, would she have been caught and gotten in trouble about it? Probably not.

But then what does it matter to register a copyright? It only matters if you have to enforce it. If someone decides to use images from Kris Kashtanova's comic as an album cover or in their book, she finds out and wants to exercise her copyrights . . . then it will have come out that she didn't create them.

You could still lie, but even if you're not caught, you're still lying. But even if you kept lying . . . your computer records could get subpoenaed to find prompts or files generated by AI. And it would be incredibly difficult to cover your tracks and delete everything, since AI generates electronic files, which leave an electronic paper trail. Even if you delete everything from your computer, it's running through servers and networks. It's not *not* discoverable.

How far do you want to lie? It might seem profitable at first. Look at the FTX guy. For some period of time he was really winning on paper. He was a media darling. He had a little place in the islands. But it all caught up to him. If you are dishonest in business, eventually your dishonesty will catch you and nobody will do business with you. If you lie to investors, that's a problem. They have recourse against you. People can sue you.

And in the long run? I see this as sinking everybody to the lowest level of quality. Where's your unique value proposition? Who's going to care about your book, graphic novel, or album if it's the same as ten other books or albums people used AI to generate? Someone is going to read it and say to themselves, "Hey, I've read this before." But now your name is on it. Who's going to care about the next thing you do?

At this point, you're not a content creator, you're just a prompter. Or just "promptrash," as I like to call them.

I came up with that term inspired by the name "patent trolls" developed by lawyers for Intel. Originally, it referred to anyone who dared to sue Intel for patent infringement, but it quickly became applied to companies that didn't have any operations but just owned patents to enforce.

Promptrash is my take on that. There's no original content; it's just generative AI drawing from the internet. It's all substantially finite. And while it's growing, most of what's growing is prompt generated. Pretty soon, the level of similarity increases and the level of originality goes down.

Why shame people like that? It's basically lying. It's someone who isn't being productive but just faking it. When ChatGPT emerged, you saw this in marketing. Everyone started sounding exactly the same, and people could spot it immediately.

When there's technology that allows for more creation and more distribution, what ends up happening is often the vast majority of new users are of absolute lowest quality. There's no resonance, there's no sales, there's no commercial viability. An ungodly number of books, for example, are self-published and posted on Amazon every day. And that was true even before AI.

What else will happen? AI is going to be deployed to weed through promptrash. If you use AI to generate your résumé or your website, there will be AI on the employer side, or on the customer side, that will review and filter out stuff. Maybe it'll give originality ratings.

Is It Possible to Copyright, Patent, or Otherwise Hold Intellectual Property Rights to an AI?

Of course!

If you think about applications of AI across industries, then there are many, many, many patents that are already issued, which means there are rights to exclude others where the claims cover the use of AI for various functions.

It might be the real-time analysis of health-care medical records. Or real-time traffic analytics and route guidance. So if someone has issued patents with claims that cover the use of AI to perform a function, then the owner of the IP rights could have the rights to shut down other AI that are applied in the same way. These claims can be used to shut down other companies' deployment of AI technology. AI patents are pretty powerful, and there's a lot to navigate. It's a minefield. But on the other hand, you might then be able to use AI to identify free space, what *isn't* covered in patent claims.

If you have a patent that has claims that cover the use of AI to monitor market activity in real time and either recommend or automatically allocate capital into different accounts or markets, you could keep others out. You would be the one place that companies would want to go to for this service.

It's also very possible you could develop an AI on your own and, not being aware of what's out there, start working with that AI . . . and then a couple of years later receive a cease-and-desist notice because someone has seen your website and found that your AI functions exactly like their claims. Then you either pay them a percentage of all your high-speed transactions or you're shut down, litigation ensues, you make a deal, you settle, and so on.

You still have to think about clearance. But if you operate outside the US, in these less patent-heavy countries, these are interesting markets for you. You could have an AI for telemedicine based in Ghana that monitors public health situations and sends out alerts via cell phone, say.

But what about the output? Does this mean that if you own the AI you create, you own the copyright to what it creates?

You still have to look at the different forms of IP. If the AI generates a data output, and you want to copyright register the data, that's a no. The outputs of AI that are IP protected may not themselves be IP protectable.

Let's use an art example. I love Refik Anadol's work. He's beyond extraordinary, and so is his art, but his art is all AI generated. If he wanted to, he could file patents on *how* he has ingested all the art or all the architecture that humanity has ever had and then *how* he directs the AI to freely make associations and render visuals on a screen. The art it generates? Not copyright registrable.

Are Data That AI Generates Protected by IP Laws?

The short answer is that they can be, as trade secrets.

But they can also be patentable. Real-time data analytics with feedback or any command-and-control activity, real-time analytics in a system with outputs or interactive user interfaces . . . those may be patentable subject matter and thus IP protectable there.

This is why big data companies are leading in AI—they get more data out of it. And the more data they have, the better trained their AI.

I can put Tesla down as an example of a company that's doing this well. It's probably because they have so much data from all the cars that are out on the road. They could have patents that cover analytics on that data for predictive charge demands on the electric power grid. So depending on where their network of cars is on the move, they could be predictive as to any of their superchargers and what the effect on the electric power grid will be if they end up arriving at the same time.

That kind of data would be hugely important. You could make the electric power grid more robust from just the car data. When we added smartphones in the way that we did in the United States, it added 30 percent more demand on the power grid. Think about gaming devices and everything else. Adding electric cars at the pace we currently are has strained the power grid, but I think that data analytics would be able to alleviate that and could be managed in a much more efficient way without creating new power plants.

But for a lot of companies, it's going to be combining different data sources that are valuable to the company but aren't integrated in real time to give insights about their business. If you're in supply chain management, you may need to be tracking public data from three different sources, and nobody else is combining that. Or it could be weather data plus activities in entertainment that may predict activity at your car wash. Or tell you that you need to bump up staff at your restaurant.

There's a lot that we see in venture capital and investing to help make decisions in a way that saves time and energy and has a better likelihood of return if you're monitoring what's happening across all the industries of the companies you invest in.

Are IP Rights Even Worth It?

The first mover doesn't necessarily win. If it's a race to file, just because you have the patent, just because you get the protection, just because you get the copyright, doesn't mean you're going to win. It doesn't mean you're going to be the biggest or the best. A multibillion-dollar company can rip off all your stuff, and they can get away with it. So is it even worth it?

Yes, IP rights are worth it, and I'm not just saying that because I'm an IP attorney.

This was said about software in the mid-2000s, when the *State Street* case provided that software was now patentable subject matter. A *lot* of people were saying, "Forget it. With software everything moves too quickly. It's not meaningful to have patents on software." Okay, then *you* don't file.

But how many software companies—big ones—file patents? They *all* do.

I hear the same argument from smaller companies. "I don't have to even think about patenting our SaaS or platform as a service offering, even if it includes AI. It's too much out there." But what do you want to do as a small company? You want to be acquired. Your exit-wealth event is acquisition. Companies won't care about you, but they will care about your IP asset quality and keeping their competition out.

Let's even go beyond AI. Let's look at quantum computing. Who are the two big guys leading the way on quantum computing? IBM and Google. Do you think they care about patents in quantum computing? Of course they do. Don't take my word for it; research the patent data, which will confirm their leading positions by date and number of patents and patent applications. So if you're a little start-up trying to do whatever you're trying to do with quantum computing, what can you do to ensure your relevancy in this emerging area of technology? You file patents. Do you think anyone might care about you or step on you? Sure, it's possible.

But as long as that person stepping on you has a competitor, the first big guy stepping on you could be crushed by the second one. If they compete with each other, if there's more than one big competitor, or even some midsize competitors to one huge one . . . the advantage of exclusive rights gets bigger in the hands of a bigger company.

If it's a valuable market—and AI is a valuable market—you should be filing patents. It's one of the indicators we think is important. And patent data shows us that companies are filing patents related to AI. In 2022, almost 65 percent of all patents issued in the US were software-related inventions, which includes AI.

"Patents are not important anymore?" I guess somebody has to tell all the companies who are participating in our patent system, then. The pace of patent-filing continues to increase. And if a majority of those are software related . . . then you know some of them are about AI.

IP rights in AI are still important, and it takes a long time to change laws.

Can AI Improve the Commercial Success of IP?

Unequivocally yes.

The commercial success of most IP is . . . not that great. Upward of 95 percent of patents have no commercial impact. Patents often don't go anywhere for many reasons, for definable reasons, though most people don't realize that. They think a patent on its own is like a lottery ticket. It's a piece of paper that's probably worthless, but it has a chance of being worth a lot.

Can AI somehow improve the odds in your favor? Can AI make IP more efficient, more effective, and more valuable? Not just in commercial impact or deployment but in improving the stats? In making it *more* likely to be commercially viable?

Yes. Our own Patent Forecast software uses AI to help analyze the quality of patents, do patent assessment, and understand the proximity of patents to each other—the context, if you will—that relates to the value of IP assets individually. A lot of times, it's not a single patent but a cluster of patents that go well together. You fill the gaps in your strategy and have a more fortified portfolio that gives you stronger exclusive rights in a hot market. AI can be helpful for identifying high-value patent assets to buy, identifying the quality of the assets, and assessing infringement.

There's a great area for deployment of AI for improving monetization of patents. But in a way, you might think it's doing the opposite. There could be AI deployments for identifying ways to invalidate patents by identifying prior art. It can certainly improve the success rates of validation.

It could also be used to identify companies that might have the greatest interest in acquiring your IP. Finding companies who will care about your IP and want to pay you for your patent rights. AI could identify companies with similar documentation or who have gaps in their portfolio that your patents fit like a key.

Are There Limits to AI?

Yes.

One thing that is limiting about AI is the datasets it deploys onto. If it's something like OpenAI, which layers on the internet, that's a huge limitation. If all the AI brain can see is the internet, there's a lot of content that's not on there that's probably more important to draw from.

Another limit of AI is being able to find solutions to unique needs people have that are emotive, or difficult to express in quantifiable measures. Because of that, I think AI is not really capable of being your friend or giving you counseling or advising in a way that human beings can do.

We think differently. Some may argue with me on this, but most of AI is still very linear in terms of how it does analytics. Humans, on the other hand, have the capacity to imagine and dream in ways that are not linear. Our minds function subconsciously in a way that we don't even completely map out.

It's the same reason humans are far better at art. People see and recognize beauty differently. When someone sees something beautiful, they're not thinking linearly. It's an emotive, intuitive thing. And that human intuition is unique to people, and I don't think machines are going to get that anytime soon. Scott Adams, creator of the *Dilbert* comic, shared on Twitter (now called X):

> [H]umans will only care about "art" (including opinion) when they know it came from a human.
>
> That's because art is an extension of our mating instinct. We don't separate the art from the artist because the triggering aspect of art is that it signals talent. Example: If AI made the Mona Lisa, it would be worth a nickel.[13]

These are things we can't easily articulate, and unless we put chips in our brains and there's a way to pull those inarticulate experiences out, AI won't be able to grasp that.

People talk about replacing lawyers with AI, but can you replace them in terms of negotiating? Finding resolutions for disputes is something even humans have a hard time doing, but it is possible. And the more you can think about what's motivating the other person, then the better you can come up with potential negotiated settlements, or alternatives to litigation or ongoing disputes.

But even if you had an AI trained on successful and unsuccessful negotiation transcripts . . . it's not merely words. Even if you could combine the visual cues, and maybe something more like sensor data about heart rate or other biometric data . . . I don't think it would change much. Because if you had an AI trained on all that and both sides are using it? It's still going to come down to what the people want.

---

13 - Scott Adams, "More evidence of my assertion that humans will only care about 'art' (including opinion) when they know it came from a human," Twitter, November 28, 2023, 8:24 a.m., https://twitter.com/ScottAdamsSays/status/1729491534045995105.

One trend that is sort of concerning to me is that we've gone from having to do the research physically, in libraries with card catalogs where you needed some effort and creativity to find what you were looking for, to convenience of not having to make the effort. The results are less valuable.

It may make it more efficient, but we've gone from having experiences finding things to "just tell me the answer." And I wonder if that will make our appetite for challenges lower. And we lose the fact that we discover things as we explore. AI doesn't really explore. It doesn't have spontaneous discovery.

Maybe Refik Anadol's *Unsupervised* is exploring in a way, but does it appreciate the hallucinations? This is what I think is limited, the machine's "imagination." As humans, we can get out of the normal, linear pattern of thinking. And that's helpful for solving problems in new ways.

CHAPTER 8

HOW TO LEVERAGE AI WITHIN YOUR BUSINESS AND STILL HAVE INTELLECTUAL PROPERTY

S oftware has always been a way to automate. You get all the speed and none of the maintenance since there are no physical moving parts. Everything you interface with is just that, an interface. However, AI goes beyond automating existing processes that have predetermined steps. It goes deeper and further. So an extended analysis of the ramifications of AI on business (such as this book) is incomplete without a section on automation. And this chapter is that.

My very first career, before going into law and before working as a US patent examiner, was new product development in an industrial setting. I was an engineer. An early learning from that work was what the processes were in the first place. Specifically: *How do you document the steps in every stage of manufacturing a new product so it can be made consistently and with high quality by confirming every step as well as all related sets of equipment for every step of the process?* The result is everything produced at a consistent quality. It's doing the same thing, the same way, over and over without deviation. In a word, automation.

At that job, we not only checked output from the end of the assembly line, we also peered into the progress along the way at each step, turn, handoff, and transition. And to do that, we had to know what each step, turn, handoff, and transition was. So do you, in your business, if you are to benefit from automation. We all want consistent industry-standard quality that also aligns with the expected and specific, well, *specifications*. That way your product works the way you say it does.

Fast-forward a few years to the mid-1990s, when I worked as a patent examiner. All the work was manual; to do prior research, we had to physically search documents. And so when you do that, and the document's not where it should be in the library, you can't find it. That is frustrating to say the extreme least.

Then we moved to digital. This changed everything. The data was now available online, so documents no longer went missing. All information was searchable. Today, at Neo IP, we do our work according to a protocol, informed by data that is now available online. We don't need to drone on about the specifics, so let's just say that leveraging digital automation makes filing with the patent office through Neo IP much, much easier than the alternative. Because we can see if there is prior art that blocks a patent application, differentiate from that prior art, and disclose everything to the patent examiner to move the process along, all with great speed and significant ease.

But back in the late '90s when I opened my firm, electronic databases were not so convenient. They used to be microfilm and microfiche; early computerized databases were cumbersome to use. You had to think of a broad category first, then use delimiters to narrow things down more and more until you hit your target search (e.g., you had to know in advance what prior art to search for that might block your application). If you didn't run the search properly and precisely (and prophetically, ha!), you didn't know what you were missing.

But automation took a not-great process and made it great. So what can automation do for you?

And what about AI-enabled automation?

That is an interesting question.

How We Automated Prior Art Patent Research

When we began automation efforts early on at Neo IP, we realized we still reviewed too many things ourselves. So I asked myself, "At what point is human intelligence necessary versus artificial intelligence?" And that was before AI was the industry we know and love and hate and fear it is today. I realized that if we could document what we considered when we made specific choices on various client projects and the tasks therein, then we could teach the machine to make those choices. We could . . . automate.

When developing or working with artificial intelligence, you have to teach the machine the way you teach a person. And just as people identify patterns the more they're taught similar material over and over, machines recognize patterns, too. They just do that faster than any human (we know of) can. After that, the system can make decisions based on those patterns, plus its training data. So we developed our own software—Patent Forecast—to automate the creation of our patent applications in a consistent way across the areas of science and technology.

Here's why we automated this broad set of tasks specifically: Newer inventions have a *lot* of prior art behind them, so there would be more manual effort to review quite literally decades of potentially blocking patents. But when we automated this workflow to speed it up, then infused artificial intelligence to analyze the findings and help make decisions, a formerly weeks-long process became nearly instantaneous. Again, this was possible because I realized that this prior art research was a consistent, teachable, and deployable process across any scenario, any company, any client, and any invention.

Patent Forecast wasn't my first automation-meets-AI effort, however. The previous version of that SaaS was called Neopatents. My team built the algorithm based on evolutionary principles to help automate the classification process. In building this, we considered the same factors that human analysts use for making decisions about classifying or categorizing. All documents (such as those detailing how the invention works and how it's sufficiently differentiated from prior art) were clustered or grouped according to their relationships with each other and with their classification. On top of that, the groups were configured into visualizations that made analysis and explanations easier.

We took this further with Patent Forecast, a software that also lets us input a disclosure, some text about a given invention, and suggested categories. We don't have to decide keywords and components anymore; the AI "looks" for those. But all eventual machine learning–driven suggestions are based on data from decades of our own research, analysis, and visualization with both the old Neopatents algorithms and good old human decision-making. Software simply accelerates the process and facilitates the work of the analyst, who can spend more time on the custom stages of any project.

We've also moved into use of AI that transforms initial input on any subject into the search query and categorization. So now the AI is also doing some of the work that analysts had to do manually by using data emergence to identify signals, determine trends, and spot anomalies or outliers, suggesting patent quality based on indicators that once required 100 percent human intervention and interpretation.

Now, reading all of this, you might be wondering how you can do the same—how you can turn weeks-long tedious processes into work that is just *done* in mere minutes.

Well, that might not be entirely possible for your company in all instances. And yet it might. Let's find out. To do that, we have to do our documentation. And by the way, that, too, can be helped with AI.

Documenting Your Process, Too

Before you write anything down about the way you do business, you have to visualize the flow, because you're not just automating workflows, you're (we hope) going to also be putting artificial intelligence in it, too. You first have to know what the flows are before you can prioritize what's most important, where's the most value, and where delays can happen. And most of the time, a machine can be taught these things; it's just a matter of how much data you have. And the great thing about patents and trademarks? There's a *lot* of data in this industry for the taking. Perhaps there is in yours, too.

The more of it you can start with, the better. Consider autonomous driving, a technological process where you're receiving data from myriad sensors in the real world, from real roads. The more available information there is, from road conditions to traffic and so on and so on and on, the more reliable and consistent any machine-made decision will be. It's like learning to play a new sport or instrument. The more you know about how to play, the more options are available to you; the more range you have as you practice. And ultimately, the better the output will be.

You're probably somewhat familiar with Tesla Motors, the brainchild of Elon Musk, known for building cars that have self-driving features. That said, they still warn you that you must remain fully attentive when using those features. As a Tesla owner myself, I've noted how they update and provide improvements, and their approach is unique: they use all the cars they have on all roads worldwide. Talk about *data*. Each individual Tesla car in the US sends a terabyte's worth of driving data per day back to the company for analysis. Many of these vehicles are on the same roads traveling around, day after day, which means they're getting reinforcement and confirmation of data in real time, in real situations. This allows Tesla's engineers via their AI to make improvements relevant to most drivers—which means improvements to each car's self-driving ability.

But most companies don't have this amount of data, especially about their clients' or customers' real-life use cases. AI only works when there's sufficient data, because this way, it has a wide variety of scenarios that allow it to make independent decisions. Tesla is not merely automating a predictable, predetermined set of steps; despite traffic laws, driving is hardly a robotic affair. It is doing something that requires real-time decision-making based on parameters that can't be predicted. That's where AI comes in—it does things that resemble what humans do, with thoughtful choices being made based on data that we have and following patterns that we have taught people.

So before you document the process, document your data. Then, document how you *analyze* that data to make decisions. How do you decide what you decide? What input do you, the human decision-maker, receive at each step, turn, handoff, and transition? All this, document first. Think of this as a step zero in the process you'll document, then automate.

What you're doing is asking yourself (or you employees), "How did you make that decision?" The answer to that question will involve data. What data? Where? How did you analyze it? How did you know how much of it to consult? What are the processes for that? Yes, there are processes within processes!

It may feel like we're getting tedious (we are). The reason is simple: You're building a digital twin of your in-house experts. No step can be skipped. No data can be lost. Everything must be disclosed. Any output is only as useful as the input.

Much like how AI image generators draw from all that is known in their training data (called a "corpus"), your AI needs material to base its "thinking" on and a process for how to "think." Take Patent Forecast again. This AI draws from all the knowns in patent applications because most inventions are new combinations of known components. The more known components we put in, the more there is to draw from, meaning the more complete, aligned, and useful the output will be for our users.

In short, data first. Make data so first it's what you do before you do anything first. It's the *first* first. Tedious? Yes. Have I made my point? Yes. What to next? Whatever we can. There's no time to waste.

When to Automate (And What Not To)

In all things automation, prioritize what's actually going to be possible. What's the cost, in terms of time and money, to do something? What do you get out of automating it?

Again the goal here is to eliminate unnecessary human work, be that labor mental or manual. I often ask clients where the AI is applied for their inventions. Can it do the same things humans do? Can it give me the results that expert attorneys can give? AI applied to workflow will automate things, but we're not only looking for full automation.

That said, do automate as much as you can, because time is money. In my industry, I really feel this. There is a race to file; there's a time pressure for patent applications and trademarks. If you're not automating, you've already lost. The best places to use AI are the things that are informed by data and where people make decisions.

But not all automation requires AI. For example, when we were developing our early patent research software, we looked at how claims were diagrammed, then wrote code that did it for us, following all the steps. Though everything was logical and clear, no one else had done it, so it was up to us. And an important part of the software was having not just the hierarchy but the content that goes into yet another level of hierarchy that was not being done at all in the early 2000s. When we surveyed everything that existed at the time, there was nothing.

Following the advice of my law firm mentor Ed Riley, we looked at the best, fastest, and cheapest options available, and what was there was not good enough. Because the best, fastest, and cheapest options were inadequate, developing our own solution would not be that difficult. Now, I didn't have to code anything myself; if I did, it would be full of bugs and other problems. Instead, I hired people that *did* know how to code, and since I knew the procedures and what needed to be done, I described it to the programmers so that they could create the architecture around it and program it.

Now, right here, I want to refer back to my previous book *The IP Miracle*, where I wrote about assignment of rights. That's what we did for all our software. We had the paperwork to confirm we owned it. Make sure you own your data, your documentation, and anything you or your team produces. Make sure all the nondisclosure and noncompete clauses and other "non" clauses are in there, plus that assignment clause, too— because anybody who builds software for you custom can sell it to your competition . . . without the paperwork. Now they have a new business, and you just taught them what it was. So whatever you automate, guarantee you'll own it.

And when working with AI, you'll probably need a specialist in the field who is familiar with all the latest techniques and tools. Make sure that you yourself are involved and that you're testing your software every step of the way. Your specialist has to break the software so that you know it can stand up to millions of users doing whatever with it, because when it's released, you will learn of issues you never caught in testing. Lucky for you, you can make patches that fix any post-release issues.

Most times, automation will be straightforward; it may take anywhere from ninety days to six months. But for AI, you have to plan on twelve to eighteen months for something custom that's trained on your datasets. But once you have it, you have it, so now you can focus your team on all the other heavy lifting. Of course, you learn something new every day, so you have to keep updating the program and updating your way of doing things.

Still Space for Human Decision-Making

But even with all the automation and AI work we've done and that you, too, will, we find that human decision-making around key aspects of our work (like patentability) is still needed. And that's even with all the data and patterns from that data we've fed and fed back into the machine. The AI we use is a large language model (LLM) since patents are assets created by words. The patents have to describe the invention in words, and a lot of the time, it's something the client discloses.

Our protocol to this day is to review the disclosure, and that review can be automated. However, we have to determine if it's clear what the invention is. Do we understand what the client is trying to say with the invention? And most times, the answer is "maybe" or "partially." So in our protocol, we have a Q&A with the client. Once we're clear on what they've submitted, we ask them how their product differs from similar ones—the unique value proposition, as I mentioned in *The IP Miracle.*

After that, the analyst translates that description into Boolean queries, which represent the most critical aspects of the invention. Most of the time, these words are predefined industry-standard terms, or they're made-up words, or they're concepts we've never heard of before. Our people are learning, which means it's not as straightforward as you might assume to run the research on. And this is where I think a lot of automated patent searches don't employ intelligence, instead preferring to pick some keywords without considering alternatives. The step of determining the query is a step that has to be done by human beings, so we see an opportunity for AI to potentially take over this role at some point.

We've done this thousands and thousands of times across different technology and science sectors, so we not only have examples of disclosure and query that were successful but queries that weren't successful either. When training these AIs, it's important to not only include data about things that worked but also about things that didn't work as well. Just like with people, AI can learn from errors, too. And because of the sheer volume of information an AI can process, it can find patterns that we never trained it to find—a benefit that goes beyond automation.

But AI has another benefit—stimulating creative uses.

AI, Automation, and Creativity

If you're stuck on something, a good way to get unstuck is to prompt an AI. Just as people do this with publicly available LLMs, you can do this with patent data, too. As long as things are categorized or referenced with words that are recognizable, they can be found.

Let's say you were looking for an attachment mechanism. Perhaps you want to know if it's permanently attaching, if the mechanism is removable, if adhesives might be involved, and so on. Just by asking the AI the question, you can get ideas about fasteners that you may not have thought of. Generative AI stimulates thinking based on past thinking of all inventions of all time, looking at the millions of solutions that have been created for various problems.

Imagine a scenario of someone who has a solution to a problem but isn't sure what material to use. Searching the internet would give this person only generic answers that won't apply to the specific situation at hand. With the AI, that person could describe their prototype and how it works, what it's meant to do, and any other relevant data they may have. Then the person can ask about things like, say, the material strength temperatures in which it needs to operate, or the cost limitations, or anything else they may not know. If you're more precise in your inquiry, you'll get better answers. Things like, *We need a new fastener that's lower cost and can be made at scale with high tolerances.* Or, *We're using this material, but it needs to be cheaper than that.* Or *We need to purchase the materials in the United States of America; who are the manufacturers?* The more detail you give it, the better your answers will be.

With solutions that exist, there are connections that extend out from that, including the inventors and the company. So if you want to hire someone or have a conversation with them, we can use generative AI to find them and get the ball rolling. Remember that generative AI is your starting point, not your final product.

It can even help you predict the future.

Predictive Analytics

When you see the data come in, a lot of things still won't be predictable, and it can be hard to read the patterns. Signals that something big is about to occur could be hidden amid meaningless noise, and no human analyst would be able to fish it out. In this area, AI would be ideal.

In our area, we often see mergers and acquisitions activity—that is, larger companies buying up smaller ones. We are trying to enhance the ability of AI to spot smaller companies that are valuable targets for M&A.

When speaking at conferences and having discussions with the guests, I often hear that the large companies just don't know that the smaller companies exist. Every company those large companies are competing with has their own war chest of patents and other IP, making them serious obstacles in the market. And the way to get valuable IP if you didn't build it yourself is to buy it.

When we at Neo IP train the AI on that pattern, we see things rising to the top that we weren't thinking about, and the narrower your prompt, the more likely you are to get good results. So we found attractive acquisition targets for Google or Apple by looking at a narrow query area—consumer sleep data—but from patents. And what we found was that wearables like Fitbit were number one in patent investment. We identified this a year before Google acquired Fitbit. Nobody had used patent data for this before.

What we notice with patent data is that a lot of people are trying to solve the same problem around the same time, and many of them have similar solutions. We see things that are similar from companies that are great distances apart worldwide, and these filings happen not just months but within weeks or days of each other. And highly technical solutions are very similar, since so much patent data and scientific research is out in the open now. Thus big companies like Google don't always need to develop their own solutions when they can buy them from these smaller companies.

This is a key way to get a competitive advantage with AI. You can use it to monitor the activity of so many companies and even predict the timing of their product releases, or maybe even how they're hiring. Just as Google has their alerts for various updates, you can have your own internal alerts if companies out in the wild are making moves that can undermine you. Just as with high-speed trading, the information processing power of AI is not something you can afford to leave behind.

It even has a role in business negotiation, should you yourself decide to buy a company. While a lot of information will be obscured, such as comparable license rates and the like, you can still ask the AI for ways to handle whatever it is you're discussing with the other company. Even if the AI hallucinates, it can point you toward the correct information when you want to confirm or correct it. You may get creative solutions that you haven't considered, since even bad ideas can spur different thinking— which is helpful in negotiations. Sometimes, you'll get something you haven't even considered.

But be careful how you use it, because misuse of generative AI has made more trouble than it's relieved.

Last Word: Don't Let It Write for You

Lazy students aren't the only ones who use generative AI services like ChatGPT. A while back, the well-known magazine *Sports Illustrated* got caught not only publishing AI-generated articles but even making up the authors of those articles, AI-made profile pictures and all. This incident,[14] not from a minor blog but from a major magazine with a real pedigree, shows the pitfalls of using AI to generate content for you. Not everything that can be automated should be, as the chapter on copyright clarified.

And it gets worse for companies who do this, because public-facing AI platforms train on the inputs, so use of them threatens the integrity of your IP rights. Let's say you wanted to write a patent application with ChatGPT instead of paying an IP attorney to do it. The result will not make sense because ChatGPT won't know how to reuse the invention. It will not teach a person of ordinary skill how to produce and use the invention, and once the examiner sees this, the application will fail. And the worst part is that you won't know for two or three years since that's how long it takes for an examiner to pick it up.

And you better hope that the attorney wrote the application themselves, because there have been more than a few attorneys getting punished for using ChatGPT or other generative AI to write their briefs before court. Using it to write your patent application will mess you up in a big way because of the amount of time it takes for an examiner to get around to it, imperiling all your IP rights. And because generative AI can be and often is wrong about things, your company's reputation will be harmed by the bad information.

And that information may not even be yours but about someone else, because AI has lots of information in its training data about all sorts of people and companies. Anything output by the AI will have to be checked, and at that point, you might as well hire a human to do the job to begin with.

This is because human creativity will be at a premium as we move further into an AI-driven world. Companies don't stay the same way all the time, simply because people come and go. This means that the information that will be processed will change as the company itself changes. The main problem with generative AI is that it's difficult to update on

---

14 - David Bauder, "Sports Illustrated Found Publishing AI Generated Stories, Photos and Authors," PBS News Hour, November 29, 2023, https://www.pbs.org/newshour/economy/sports-illustrated-found-publishing-ai-generated-stories-photos-and-authors.

the fly, and also it doesn't have a personality or style until you force it to adopt one.

People want people; that's why artists have portfolios. People can change over time, instead of adopting the robotic styles typical of AI. They want human authenticity, not just the cold perfection that a machine can give you.

Adding to that, you should check for AI use, since you could be risking not only infringing someone else by mistake but also losing any IP claim to what was published. Doing that will become more and more difficult as time goes on, since AI on the surface reduces the amount of work needed.

That said, it's not as if there's no place for AI at all. The correct thing to do nowadays is to train employees how to use it to improve their workflows while dissuading them from improper use. While using it to generate written material makes no sense, using it to seek out patterns within huge amounts of data is a valid use—for example, generating and refining search queries for the US Patent and Trademark Office. You could even use it to identify competitors. It can nudge us to follow up on emails and other communication, and it can keep us alert to what's going on around us.

Companies should inventory both their IP assets and their AI tools and ask themselves what they're using today and what works. New tools are released all the time, as evidenced by the explosion of patent applications involving AI. Whatever you taught your employees to use may become obsolete in a few months' time as your employees find new tools. You have to stay on top of all this, because it will only accelerate. People will do what makes life easier, so open discussion of AI should be a norm. Let those who have figured out how to use AI teach others the ropes.

Treat this with the urgency it requires, too. Since AI is already an important technology, all your employees need to know what's going on in the company and how to deploy it in an effective way. Because what will differentiate you is creativity in using these tools to find new ways to solve their problems and do things that a machine can't do alone. You don't want to just be using the tools to get some clean and easy result. You have to keep upskilling as you learn AI and automation.

Get serious when handling this; put it in your employee handbook: *It is not okay to do X, Y, and Z with AI software. No AI output should be passed off as human-made; we want human-generated content whenever possible.* You have to screen what gets written before it's published so that any cheating involving AI is caught and fixed. Misuse of AI can sink your reputation and harm your IP rights, so don't play around here.

Fear is a double-edged sword. On one side, it can cut your business deep. On the other, it cuts a prized path into the future so you can get there before competitors do.

Use the sword wisely.

That being said, consider how some are wielding a sword against AI learning from their creative works. Researchers at the University of Chicago have unveiled Nightshade, a new tool that allows artists to "poison" their images so that AI models cannot be trained on them.[15]

The announcement indicated that to human eyes, these poisoned images will not look any very different from the originals. But models trained on these images will learn unpredictable behaviors that will not provide outputs aligned with the prompts. By way of example, a prompt that asks for "pig flying over a field" might instead get an image of a toaster over a field.

What other poisoning could have happened with AI trainings? Should we trust AI outputs completely? Do we trust Google results or Siri or Alexa completely? We will continue to explore the AI space regularly and share results with everyone who joins our newsletter. Visit www.jinanglasgowgeorge.com now.

---

15 - Melissa Heikkilä, "The New Data Poisoning Tool Lets Artists Fight Back against Generative AI," MIT Technology Review, October 23, 2023, https://www.technologyreview.com/2023/10/23/1082189/data-poisoning-artists-fight-generative-ai/.

CHAPTER 9

███ ▌ ███ ▐▌

THE FUTURE

With the advent of AI, all industries have already begun to change, be those industries creative and artistic or mundane and manually laborious. Regardless, there will only be more change, and change that accelerates faster and faster until it feels like decades of progress happen in a week. Every week. And then a day. No stopping it now.

If your job is to work with intellectual property, to create it or protect it, these changes will affect you more than most. So the best way I can give you some semblance of a head start is to offer these four reminders—the four key takeaways from this book. Commit them to memory and take them to heart. For all that will change in the coming years, these will most likely not be among them.

AI & IP Takeaway 1: If AI Makes It, No IP Rights for You

AI is great for many things, and it will take the work out of a lot of mundane tasks. However, it is not good for inventing or authoring, no matter how good it gets. The reason is simple—IP rights can be granted only if there is human authorship, and AI is not human, so there can be no IP there. Without exclusivity, you can't build a business around what was created, because then anyone can take it and make a competing product or service. Leaving aside the ethical questions about how the training data was acquired, using AI to create the content will leave you with a bunch of data that has no value.

AI & IP Takeaway 2: You Can Use AI for Trademarks (and Brainstorming)

While AI-created works cannot be copyrighted, you can still use AI to generate trademark logos for yourself. This is because when you trademark something, it doesn't matter where it came from, only that it identifies your business. This is because the value of a trademark comes from how it's used in the marketplace and who that symbol or sign is associated with. Thus having an AI generate your logo poses no danger to your trademark rights.

But another way you can use AI is to stimulate your thinking. You may be stuck on some project, and you can ask the AI for approaches to use. Just make sure you or your team implements the changes, not the AI. And as I mentioned before, AI is great at processing information, so it can perform the appropriate research for you faster, especially if it involves huge volumes of data (like Patent Forecast does, for example). The same goes for searching. No one likes to do this sort of drudgery, so using AI to do it only comes with advantages.

AI & IP Takeaway 3: Human Creativity Is King (or Queen)

For anything creative, the value comes from the uniqueness of the human being who made it. It's not like automating the production of motor vehicles; creative projects come from a person, so taking the person out of it diminishes its value.

Notice what happens when AI-generated songs, images, and other creative works come out—they are derided as trash. But you can have this situation, too: There is a song or video that comes out that's AI generated, but it's not obvious to a casual observer. People will like it, and they'll share it around. They will talk about it and get their friends to participate. Follower counts will go up all over social media. But once it comes out that all this content was made by AI, that reputation collapses.

This is because people will feel duped—they thought they were supporting an amazing artist that no one knew about. But it turns out that the "artist" was just AI content, so the whole thing feels like you got tricked. People will walk back their support, and the brand associated with it will suffer. People will think of the brand as phony or fake, because that's how AI-generated content is seen.

Look at it this way—if you paid a lot of money for a piece of art, you're under the impression that it came from an actual artist who put hours of skill into crafting that work. However, if you find out that it was computer generated in seconds, you will feel ripped off, because you could've done that yourself with the right prompt. If something took no effort to create, it doesn't have value, no matter how elaborate it is. Thus a creative work only has value if it's created by human beings. Computers don't have a personality. Software doesn't have a personality. Since these things lack the human qualities we value, we don't value the things it puts out.

By contrast, natural resources have value because they are rare, expensive to transform into finished products, and finite. You can't just hit "generate" on a piece of software and get more oil or rare-earth metals— you need to find them, dig them up, refine them, and make useful products with them. Likewise, human-made art requires skill and time, so it will be inherently more valuable than something that can be created in seconds.

When it comes to art, the main exceptions to this will be personal brands like Refik Anadol, who has built his specific brand on AI-generated art and is open about how he uses it. On top of that, he doesn't use public-facing platforms; instead, he has a team of about a dozen people to train and refine the AI he uses to make his art pieces. He even has the support of Nvidia and Google, two big players in the AI space.

But despite Anadol's openness and honesty about how he uses the technology, AI itself will not be assigned respect. We want Siri to answer our questions right away; we don't want Siri to take our job.

AI & IP Takeaway 4: Disclose or Die

The US Copyright Office requires you to disclose AI use in the creation of something. Of all that is unlikely to change, this is far and above the unlikeliest. Human nature down through time changes at a snail's pace; the US government, at the speed of a glacier.

Oh, and as of this writing, Amazon also requires disclosure when you upload book and ebook files for self-publishing. You have to be up front about using *all* of this AI stuff, making it abundantly clear that you are putting the AI outputs together. That said, it still won't give you the copyrights to the content.

There's a distrust surrounding these machines. It's one thing if they're merely doing data processing for us, or performing some useful task that we would rather not perform ourselves. But once AI encroaches on the area where humans express themselves (like art), people get uncomfortable. And why wouldn't they? Nothing like this has existed before, and human beings fear the unknown like nothing else.

Nonetheless, there will be changes in the coming years, as questions of copyright get handled in the courts and we see the full impact of these new technologies on human employment going forward. The consensus against them may seem strong now, but that may well change as time goes on.

To stay up to date on what *is* changing, you can subscribe to our free email newsletter. You'll get weekly updates, breaking news reports, and industry-insider thought pieces so you always know what is happening and how to take action to preserve and progress your IP rights.

See you at www.jinanglasgowgeorge.com.

ABOUT THE AUTHOR

JiNan Glasgow George is recognized worldwide for her expertise in global intellectual property strategy. She is ranked among the IAM Strategy 300 World's Leading IP Strategists and has worked with the United Nations and numerous research and development labs in the United States and abroad on IP and entrepreneurship to drive measurable economic impact. Her books *The IP Miracle* and *IP in the Age of AI* are the essential reads for transforming ideas into protected intellectual property assets. Learn more at www.neoipassets.com.

BOOK DESCRIPTION

From the author of _The IP Miracle_, an eye-opening resource for securing valuable intellectual property rights in the uncertain age of AI.

IP in the Age of AI will help you protect your company's creative capital while leveraging the superproductivity of artificial intelligence—and without sabotaging your exclusive rights. Drawing from JiNan Glasgow George's thirty-plus years of experience engineering new products and helping companies globally secure strategic IP rights, this book builds on _The IP Miracle_ to bring the force multiplier of AI to your IP portfolio and innovation workflow. In an intuitive Q&A format, JiNan examines the evolving legal complexities surrounding the ever-increasing presence of AI in common business activities, from marketing to media to research and development.

Find answers on:

- The current limitations of AI for intellectual property
- How to stimulate creativity using AI without losing exclusive rights
- The legal and financial pitfalls of using AI improperly
- How to leverage AI in your company workflow
- Nonobvious ways to beat the competition using AI
- How to find the latest updates on news concerning IP and AI
- The limitations and advantages of using third-party AI tools

IP in the Age of AI asks critical questions and delivers essential answers for business in a world forever changed by artificial intelligence.